19/2/16

Malcolm — Many thanks
those years ago when ...
N. Ireland. It was a great
... you with us.    Rama.

# PSYCHIATRIC REHABILITATION
## A Psychoanalytic Approach to Recovery

*Raman Kapur*

**KARNAC**

First published in 2016 by
Karnac Books Ltd
118 Finchley Road
London NW3 5HT

British Library Cataloguing in Publication Data

A C.I.P. for this book is available from the British Library

ISBN-13: 978-1-78220-156-4

Typeset by V Publishing Solutions Pvt Ltd., Chennai, India

Printed in Great Britain

www.karnacbooks.com

# CONTENTS

# ACKNOWLEDGEMENTS

A special acknowledgement must go to those who created the foundations of Threshold in Northern Ireland, namely Ms. Elly Jansen (formerly CEO of Richmond Fellowship UK), Mr. John McCarthy (formerly assistant director, Richmond Fellowship UK and sadly now deceased), and Mr. Michael B. Weir (Threshold first director).

I acknowledge my debt to my own psychoanalyst, Dr. Christopher Holland (psychiatrist and formerly of the Tavistock Clinic and member of the Scottish Institute of Human Relations) who brought me through my early years of training in London. He was to become Threshold's own psychoanalyst from its inception in 1990.

I am deeply grateful to my parents, Dwarka Nath and Phula Rani Kapur, who brought our family to settle in Northern Ireland in the 1950s, to escape the unrest in their homeland of India.

My hope is that this book recognises their support to me and makes a small, if modest contribution to the care of people with severe mental illness.

# ABOUT THE AUTHOR

**Dr. Raman Kapur, MBE**, is a Consultant Clinical Psychologist by profession, specialising in Psychotherapy and is also the Chief Executive Officer of the mental health charity THRESHOLD, based in Belfast in Northern Ireland. He is an Associate Fellow of the British Psychological Society and he also holds an Honorary Senior Lectureship with the School of Psychology, The Queens University of Belfast and was formerly course Director of the MSc in Psychoanalytic Psychotherapy at the School. In 2012 he was awarded an MBE by the Queen for his work in providing services to people with mental illness in Northern Ireland.

# The state of mind to be rehabilitated or recovered

As a young clinical psychology trainee, my first experience of coming face to face with severe mental illness was when I inadvertently interviewed a young married woman in her mid-twenties, who had just suffered a schizophrenic breakdown. Back then, in 1980, clinical psychology trainees were not allowed to speak to such patients. It was seen as dangerous and we could only see patients suffering from dog phobia or agoraphobia. Even then, patients had to be screened by a psychiatrist before we could see them. This memory has stayed with me over my thirty years in mental health. My recollection of the interview is as follows: "I'm just plain scared out of my wits. I just want to talk to someone. These dangerous things come into my mind and take me over and I don't know what to do. Please help me,"

As a trainee, I tried my best to engage this patient in some kind of helpful conversation and I did believe my attempts to help her were successful. However, when my supervisor found out that I had dared to sit in the room with a "mad" patient, she reprimanded me and said if I ever was to do such a thing again, I would be thrown off the course. I never returned, as I had promised, to see this patient and to this day I wonder what became of her.

Without all the theoretical concepts and clinical expertise I now have at my disposal, I felt I did do my best to help this patient who felt lonely, isolated, afraid, even terrified about what was going on inside her mind. Of course, conventional psychiatric nomenclature gives patients suffering from mental health problems a diagnosis, and subsequent pharmacological or psychological treatment interventions to deal with their difficulties. The recent ICD 10 (International Classification of Diseases) and DSM—5 (*Diagnostic and Statistical Manual of Mental Disorder*) have many classifications that fit many of the signs and symptoms we see in everyday psychiatric practice. However, these classification systems singularly fail to capture the subjective experiences of the patient suffering from severe mental illness. The recent upsurge in cognitive behavioural therapy (CBT) does "what it says on the tin": addresses cognitions and behaviour with the hope that feelings will follow. The style of CBT is very much to focus on how the patient thinks through structured interventions aimed at facilitating change.

General psychotherapeutic approaches tend to address more relational and emotional elements of the patient's distress. It was these approaches that were most available to me in my first five years in clinical psychology, where I worked in primary care, acute psychiatry, and elderly severely mentally ill settings. This more general humanistic/psychodynamic approach is based on a view that if you are able to empathise with the patient and "show them the errors of their ways" or dysfunctional thinking (Kapur, 1988), changes will follow. Transactional analysis and Gestalt therapies are based on this idea with structured exercises to facilitate change. Invariably, the therapist is active with the patient, suggesting ideas or ways of thinking and feeling in a different way. Most of these psychodynamic approaches are based in the world of interpersonal psychoanalysis and the writings of psychotherapists such as Harry Stack Sullivan (1962) and Frieda Fromm-Reichmann (1950), along with the work of Irving Yalom (1970, 1983). Within this interpersonal model, the focus is very much on providing a corrective emotional experience (Frank, 1959) to the patient, whereby he is left feeling accepted and understood, with the idea of forming a therapeutic alliance (Hovarth & Greenberg, 1994) with thetherapist/patient relationship seen as the platform for positive changes.

Psychotherapy is taken as dealing with the dysfunctional relationship patterns of the patient and through an exposure to a corrective emotional experience, changes in these patterns are seen to emerge. Here the emphasis is on insight, facilitating interpersonal changes within the context of a supportive relationship, exuding the characteristics of warmth, empathy, and unconditional positive regard (Rogers, 1951). This formed the basis of my early work in psychiatry and with other patient populations (Kapur, 1987, 1988).

However, I was always uneasy about these approaches and felt I was missing something. It was this curiosity that took me into the world of London Kleinian and post-Kleinian psychoanalysis (Hobson & Kapur, 2005; Hobson, Patrick, Kapur, & Lyons-Ruth, 2013; Kapur, 1991, 1999). I was appointed as senior clinical psychologist at Shenley Hospital in London from 1987 to 1990, with responsibility for the semi-secure and acute psychiatric wards. Little did I know that my job was to replace several senior Kleinian psychoanalysts who ran the Woodside Therapeutic Community (Sohn, 1985) after the post-Laingian work of Cooper (1986). What a psychic shock!

After managing considerable conflicts between clinical psychologists and psychoanalysts, I found an opportunity to discover a model of the severely mentally ill mind that I thought could address this "missing link" in my professional work.

A necessary precondition to discovering this missing link was to undertake my own personal analysis (up to three times per week) over three years. As my interest was not the "worried well" I decided not to go down the formal route of psychoanalytic trainings which in reality would have taken me out of my NHS patient population. Also, as cited in my two main pieces of research on psychoanalytic therapy (Kapur, 1993, 1998) there is no training course in the UK to help mental health clinicians work with severe mental illness. Within my own psychoanalytic experience, I found those in most need got least psychoanalytic help.

As Segal (1986) reports, and as Hobson (2013) so clearly elucidates with "everything happens in the first session", so I found this to be the case. Whatever my own material, what struck me was that my analyst kept very still and only spoke when he had something to say about my "state of mind", particularly in relation to him. This was a huge contrast to the many psychotherapeutic approaches that I had been exposed to and it has shaped my work up to this day. This style is significantly different to most clinical psychology interventions and also other psychoanalytic approaches (Gomez, 1989). It was the focus on my "state of mind" that paid *wholesome* attention to subjective or intrapsychic processes, in a very simple and powerful way.

M. J. Horowitz (1987) has used the phrase "state of mind" to analyse changes in individual psychotherapy. This phrase, I think, can best capture the subjectivity of those suffering from severe mental illness, as described by my first patient earlier. Also, there is much debate within my own profession on "formulation" (British Psychological Society/ Division of Clinical Psychology, 2013) where it is given as a position statement:

> The DCP is of the view that it is timely and appropriate to affirm publicly that the current classification system as outlined in DSM—5 and ICD 10, in respect of functional psychiatric diagnosis, has significant conceptual and empirical limitations, consequently there is a need for a paradigm shift in relation to the experiences that these diagnoses refer to, towards a conceptual system which is no longer based on a "disease" system.

Many in my own profession (Bentall, 2004; Boyle, 2002; Kinderman, 2014) are anti-diagnosis of any nature, with an emphasis more on formulation (Johnstone & Ballos, 2006) where there is a description of the individual distress along with a description of aetiology and possible treatment interventions. However, the internal world of the patient is not the raison d' être of this paradigm and potentially fails to address the subjectivity and deeper experience of a patient with severe mental illness. Also, and an issue which I believe is extremely relevant for the real world of psychiatric illness, most patients can feel things are being "done to them", rather than waiting to see how their internal worlds are emerging. I would suggest by simply capturing this "state of mind" in everyday practice, it could synergistically complement diagnostic and formulation paradigms to help offer the patient a comprehensive understanding of his mental illness.

Hobson (2013) makes a similar point. I think it is important to bear in mind that the psychoanalytic perspective that both he and I speak from places the utmost importance on the mental health professional being a patient on the couch not only to learn from experience of the psychoanalytic process but also to know what it feels like to be in the vulnerable position of being a patient. As such, in the whole range of psychotherapies, this particular Kleinian model raison d'être means it is vital for analysts to be a patient themselves in order to be able to treat a patient. He writes:

> Perhaps I am ducking something. This is that, as a patient, I know I would hate to be given a formulation. To be formulated, whether or not I had a part in the formulating process, is not what I had come for. If there are rational and civilized reasons for giving a formulation—and certainly there are—I would offset these with something captured by T. S. Eliot/Alfred Prufrock: "… and when I am formulated, sprawling on a pin/When I am pinned and wriggling on a wall/Then how should I begin/To spit out all the butt ends of my days and ways?" (p. 118)

He goes on to write of the limitations that occur in psychiatry with general diagnostic formulations and then makes an important point which is consistent with the ideas in this text: "I would have thought that the best way to capture something of the individual person is to give a small but detailed portrait of the way this person relates to a therapist in a consultation" (p. 118).

## State of mind evidence

Hobson (2013) describes three classes of evidence that make up an understanding of someone's life. First, there are the facts around age, gender, employment, etc., followed by reports of what a patient may disclose through his personal history and his reported good or bad experiences of his "significant others". It is his third class of evidence that is of particular interest in capturing a patient's state of mind. He writes:

> These are facts of how the patient engages with the therapist, as well as with the patient him/herself. Of course, one might say that such relations too, express unconscious phantasy (where "phantasy" refers to a largely unconscious inner world of personal relations). And indeed they do. But there is something special about the nature of the evidence on which one draws to arrive at judgements about interpersonal engagement that is special, whether or not one is focused on the "unconscious phantasy" part of what is happening.

> The evidence is special by virtue of its source in the unique qualities of "inter-subjective engagement". At the next most basic level, we apprehend and come to understand the nature of persons' and people's mental states through our emotional engagements "with" persons and the attitudes they express. (pp. 12–13)

In psychoanalytic parlance, this would be termed the "free associations" of the patient which are understood and received by the therapist/analyst. It is these spontaneous patient utterances that constitute the material for the understanding and capture of the state of mind of the patient; for the therapist or mental health professional to be quiet and gather the evidence and material simply from allowing the patient to speak first.

Some examples from my own clinical practice, in the formality of a psychotherapy setting or in a ward or in an outpatient clinic, can provide powerful insights into the patient's state of mind.

## Three states of mind

### 1. Visit to a mental health project

"So you're Dr. Kapur. I think you can cure me."

From day to day working in general psychiatry to the formalised setting of psychoanalytic work, the patient will always be emotionally alive in what he does with others. Yet, very little attention is paid to the impact of deeper processes on staff and in return, how staff deal with these processes (Kapur, 1991). However, even brief comments from the patient can offer some powerful insights into "who is doing what to whom".

In this particular utterance the patient is expecting me to be God and cure her from severe mental illness. This, potentially, is her predominant state of mind. She gazes into me as if I am some Indian god (Kapur, 2008a) who can take her illness away and provide her with a peace of mind she does not have. Of course, a natural reaction on my part would be to respond to this request for a miracle by offering all sorts of "psychological magic". Alternatively, if I suffered from faulty narcissism, I could participate in some deluded phantasy that I could indeed cure her of her illness and bask in a mad idealisation of my powers.

However, another ordinary and more thoughtful response would be to realise the depth of her despair, that she is so desperate to be relieved of her inner torment that she wants me to perform a miracle. So, perhaps, I could inform the staff of this insight in order to help them to react in an ordinary way, to take seriously her despair, rather than in an extraordinary way to offer the promise of a cure and then feel inadequate when this fails. In doing so, the patient could then engage in "ordinary hard work" to tune into the patient's state of mind (Lucas, 2009) and offer a response that takes seriously her desperation to get better but, what is important, then embark on the work of helping the patient engage with the ordinary activities in the service and undertake the small, but significant steps required for her rehabilitation, such as engaging in support and care plans and vocational rehabilitation, facilitating more independent living.

By keeping this predominant "state of mind" in place the mental health worker can respond more accurately to the needs of the patient, not feel inadequate when even best efforts fail, and provide realistic opportunities for the patient to be rehabilitated and recover from the impact of severe mental illness on his life.

## 2. First outpatient appointment

"I have had so many problems with depression, I have tried so many medications and physical treatments and I've learnt to put up with things. Now, you're my last chance."

In this first interchange the patient can relocate his "depressed self" into the psychotherapist's hands to "fix". The recipient of this state of mind is in the role of being the human anti-depressant for this patient and is faced with the pressure of feeling that he is the patient's last hope. It may also be that this meets an element of the depressed self in the psychotherapist and potentially, the recipient of this state of mind is faced with a momentary decision as to what to do, "How do I deal with feelings of depression and sadness in my own inner life?"

In the particular theoretical and clinical framework adopted in this text (see Chapter One and Hobson, 2013) this "moment of depression" would be "thought about, considered and then articulated" to the patient with a comment such as: "I think you feel that if I can't quickly remove this feeling of depression from you, that coming to see me would be a waste of time and I would be yet another failed treatment for you." When I did offer such a comment to the patient, it opened up a whole plethora of memories and feelings to do with past failures, unrealistic hopes and expectations that were not met, and feelings of deep inadequacy. By offering some thought to this state of mind, some movement was made in the internal world of this patient, which led to some "lifting" of the heaviness of memories and experiences in his mind that left him so depressed. The ongoing and future psychotherapy was characterised by this working and reworking of this state of mind through thinking about and verbalising what was happening between both therapist and patient, rather than entering into a reactive anti-depressant physiology/psychology that potentially would end in the failure and defeat of further unrealistic hopes for a "quick fix".

### 3. Ongoing psychotherapy

"What I feel you want me to do is address the anger ... I think that if I addressed the anger you would feel that I can carry on, but what I can't get you to realise is that I don't want to address my anger. I'm afraid of you saying to me 'Roisin, it is eleven o'clock, it is time to go, get out through the door.' You can switch off ... I can't ... I would be out of control if you said to me go away at eleven o'clock. I can't see it doing me any good. I can only see it destroying me, like a self-destruction. I don't want that. I have been through enough pain in my life. A lot of it I have caused myself, just in my own negative thoughts. I haven't got a lot of self-confidence. I still don't, but I am slowly starting to say to myself, if people can't accept you for what you are, whatever that may be, that's tough, that's their problem not yours, and I'm really applying that to my parents. For once I am starting to stand up and if I feel like saying no, I say no. I'm not downright rude but whatever the situation is that comes up, whether it's right or wrong. I don't know, that remains to be seen, but I feel for once I am standing on my own two feet. I am doing what I want to do, most of the time, not always. Whatever I do it's my consequences, it's me that has to be responsible for it and I want to do that. I do honestly feel we have come to the end of the road."

This would be representative of a typical psychotherapy session, whether it is a first session, as it was in this excerpt, or an ongoing psychotherapy. Whatever the temporal location of this excerpt, several themes can be inferred from the patient's statement of mind:

- The patient recognises that she struggles with strong emotions, particularly anger, but is terribly worried that she will be "switched off" and cast out by the therapist.
- She is frightened of relinquishing any self-control that she has developed over what seems to have been a troubled and painful life.
- She also recognises the effect of perpetual negative thoughts on her self-confidence and tries pragmatically to "accept who you are, what you are, people can like it or lump it".
- She talks about standing up for herself as a way of defending herself but also potentially to take some pride in herself.
- She believes that personal responsibility is a good idea but worries it could not be her saviour but the "end of the road" of her efforts to feel better.

Clearly, there are lots of themes to pick up on and it is difficult to decide which is the predominant "state of mind". My own view would be to "distil" her state of mind down to this comment:

"For a long time you have managed difficult feelings by yourself and you would like a way to get some help from me or others, to stand up to the overwhelming negativity that can cause so much distress. However, depending on another human being to do this is frightening, as depending on others has not always been good for you."

So here I am simply trying to capture the predominant state of mind, particularly in relation to me, to give her some understanding of the intensity of feelings she struggles with.

## Rehabilitation and recovery

The purpose of this book and indeed the purpose of the clinical practice of psychoanalysis rests on the efficacy of human intervention. Most of us regard the provision of a good object/breast/ mother, bearing what is unbearable to the infant and empathising with the predicament of that infant and providing appropriate nourishment and help to deal with that experience and develop knowledge as essential for growth. The bond that develops of being valued and concerned with each other, can be strong enough to cope with internal and external events and is the bedrock of human meaningfulness. The combined love and concern of both parties and its development give ground for faith and appreciation in living—one is not alone and human endeavour is the main source of finding and being meaningful.

The aim of this book is in line with the aim of those analysts who consider that the recapturing of the early good object relationship is essential to acquire the strength to meet the vicissitudes of life. (Brenman, 2006, pp. xxiv–xxv)

So writes Eric Brenman, a senior psychoanalyst in his book entitled *Recovery of the Lost Good Object*. Clearly this could never be the aim of the recovery and rehabilitation of work with severely mentally ill patients that this book addresses. However, it is the recovery of some aspect of "goodness" that is central to the rehabilitation process, whether it be in the consulting room or a psychiatric hospital setting. It is the latter that is of interest in this text which I would like to formulate as follows:

A mind damaged by severe mental illness is in fragments. Chaos reigns and there are no boundaries. The patient is often caught in similar chaotic, boundary-less or over-boundaried atmospheres. Badness is everywhere. To recover from this, an atmosphere needs to be created that is boundaried, ordered, and conveys a sense of empathy, concern, and understanding. If the patient feels sufficiently "thought about" then he can be helped to recover to a better state of mind and rehabilitated into the community.

While the therapeutic community movement (which I will refer to later in Chapter Two) has made significant efforts to address the issue of maximising settings to aid recovery (e.g., Campling, Davies, & Farquharson, 2004), there has been little written on maximising the therapeutic potential of everyday psychiatric environments to address the emotional or subjective aspects of recovery and rehabilitation. While the agency I manage, Threshold, is part of the therapeutic community network in the UK (the Community of Communities initiative of the Royal College of Psychiatrists), I believe that not enough attention is paid in the therapeutic community movements to the minutiae of what happens in the atmospheres in the day-to-day running of such settings. This text proposes a comprehensive clinical model that addresses all the needs of the patient with severe mental illness, particularly focusing on how each individual state of mind is managed in a therapeutic atmosphere designed to maximise hope and independence, the twin paramount aims of the recovery model in rehabilitative psychiatry (Slade, 2009).

I will now review contemporary psychiatric definitions of recovery and then, particularly referring to Brenman's (2006) guide, set the scene for the rationale and content of the following chapters of this book.

Ralph and Corrigan (2005) propose three definitions of recovery:

> 1. Recovery is a natural occurring phenomenon. Some people who meet diagnostic criteria for serious mental illness are able to overcome their disabilities and enjoy a full life in which their life goals are accomplished without any kind of treatment.
> 2. As with other medical illnesses, people can recover from mental illness with proper treatment. Others who do not enjoy spontaneous recovery from mental illness are able to achieve a similar state of goal attainment and life satisfaction as a result of participating in a variety of services.
> 3. Recovery reintroduces the idea of hope in understanding serious mental illness … it means that even though a person is diagnosed with schizophrenia or other serious psychiatric disorder, his or her life need not be limited by institutions. (pp. 4–5)

Slade (2009) suggests that mental health professionals see the second definition as clinical recovery, whereas users and carers of services prefer the first or third definition. However, whatever the definition, the central theme is that there is an experience of moving on, often having a greater trust in the atmosphere and people engaged with the patient and of things changing for the better. So for this to happen, as Brenman (2006) suggests, there has to be trustworthiness in the goodness of others that concern, understanding, and help are at the core of their beliefs. This is the central message of this book and the ideas proposed to create an emotional architecture that maximises the goodness in the air the patient finds himself in. The text will use the model of the traditional consulting room to point to elements of the atmosphere that need to be put in place, along with other critical external world aspects from accommodation to structured activities, to create a setting that maximises hope and independence.

Theoretically and clinically, this book will draw from psychoanalysis, rehabilitative psychiatry, and clinical psychology to formulate ideas and practices that have been tested out in the real world of running and managing a voluntary mental health agency (Kapur, 2008b, 2009). As such, it will bring to life ideas in the reality of a severely mentally ill patient leaving a psychiatric ward and entering into an atmosphere "designed by humans for humans". Its predominant theoretical model will be in contemporary psychoanalytic object relations (e.g., Hobson, 2013), but it will integrate this with the reality of psychiatry and social care.

Chapter One will outline the theoretical underpinnings of this book which is based on the individual and group psychoanalytic practice of the Kleinian and post-Kleinian object relations school where their ideas have been applied to people with severe mental illness (Lucas, 2009). This is the theoretical and clinical backbone of this book. While I will refer to other allied fields in psychotherapy, psychiatry, and clinical psychology, the overarching framework is based on the work of Melanie Klein and Wilfred Bion, which I have commented upon and studied elsewhere (e.g. Kapur, 1993, 1998, 2014).

Chapter Two will differentiate between the conventional therapeutic community ideas and the focus on therapeutic atmospheres which is the central idea of this book. Some reference will be made to therapeutic environments as they are described in the general psychiatric literature.

Group processes will be covered in Chapter Three, from community meetings (large groups) to small groups, as well as covering group psychotherapy theorists such as Bion, Foulkes, and Yalom.

Chapter Four will particularly focus on how the individual patient's state of mind can be captured in individual work whereby the patient has "private" experience of being contained and understood.

Equipping staff in residential and non-residential settings with the expertise to help severely mentally ill patients will be described in Chapter Five. Using the idea of Maslow's hierarchy of needs, training will be described which attends to the physical and emotional needs of the patient.

In Chapter Six, process and outcome findings will be reported in psychotherapeutic settings for severely mentally ill people. Also, measures will be suggested that could capture the atmospheres in therapeutic settings along with outcome measures that can potentially also capture personal and clinical aspects of recovery.

In Chapter Seven, I will describe the advantages and disadvantages of inviting external consultants to contribute to the work with severely mentally ill patients. Thoughtful use of such inputs can enrich the quality of a service but the employment of consultants whose values are incongruent with the values and culture of the organisation can create havoc with disastrous consequences.

Management and leadership issues are rarely addressed in the real world of mental health and social care. Often trainings are offered in the virtual reality of a work setting which can take away from the reality of managing difficult relationships and emotions where there are huge consequences of staff acting out their own difficulties. Chapter Eight (revised version of a published paper, Kapur, 2009) details the management of very "live" events which can "make or break" an organisation.

Chapter Nine details critical employment issues that are rarely, if ever, addressed in the psychoanalytic literature. The implications of disciplinary and grievance issues are discussed in how they affect the patient and the overall state of mind of the organisation.

I conclude the book by suggesting that any mental health setting can transform its atmosphere through carefully considering and implementing these ideas. By doing this, the reader can begin to address the emotional life of the patient, which all too often is lost in the drive to "make patients better".

## CHAPTER ONE

# Theoretical overview

"So if I depend on you, I have to give up my superior self and be a normal human being, but then I would hate you because I would have to accept you have more than me, you are worthy to depend on and I can't bear that" (patient).

T his text will take a particular approach to understanding the state of mind of a severely mentally ill patient by focusing on how the internal or emotional world of the patient relates to the helper, whether that is a health and social care worker, mental health professional, or psychoanalyst. While the theoretical framework to be described here wholly comes from psychoanalysts who follow the work of Melanie Klein and Wilfred Bion, the premise of this text is that these phenomena occur as much outside the consulting room as they do inside the consulting room. It is through informing us all and those who are helping these patients, of how these powerful internal processes impact on them, that we can build optimal therapeutic atmospheres that can best help such patients. Whatever the help, powerful processes are often activated when deeper connections or links become unearthed. For the severely mentally ill patient, the solitary world is a safe world and any human contact is met with a violent rejection.

1

I will now outline the key elements of Kleinian theory as they apply to helping people with severe mental illness and, after overviewing Melanie Klein's broad theoretical framework, I will highlight particular clinical phenomena experienced in everyday work with this patient population.

## Paranoid–schizoid functioning

"I think the dream means I have to trust you. It feels like standing on a cliff edge; ready to jump. But I don't think there is anyone there to catch me. Jumping into the void. No one there."

Melanie Klein coined the phrase "'paranoid-schizoid" attempting to highlight the depth of distrust that patients live with in their day-to-day lives. For people with severe mental illness it becomes a chasm of mistrust and as in the above quote from a patient, there often has been no one to "catch" them, to lean on, and thus disturbed and difficult thoughts and feelings have never been spoken about. In this particular theoretical framework, this is the fuel for all psychopathology, whether it is a psychotic or neurotic disorder. This underlying distrust becomes the fundamental building block for emotional life and denotes the depth and breadth of all psychopathology. In its simplest and purest form, it is unconditional trust and intimacy which creates the backbone of emotional life. Melanie Klein writes:

> The capacity for love and devotion, first of all to the mother, in many ways develops into devotion to various causes that are felt to be good and valuable. This means that the enjoyment which in the past the baby was able to experience because he felt loved and loving, in later life becomes transferred not only to his relations to people, which is very important, but also to his work and to all that he feels worth striving for. This means also an enrichment of the personality and capacity to enjoy work, and opens up a variety of sources of satisfaction. (1959, p. 258)

For Klein the "golden bullet" of a healthy personality is the capacity to have a sense of trust and ease with others. However, if this is missing, the emotional processes in the paranoid-schizoid position become the normality of everyday life. What is important is that this state of mind is characterised by emotional poverty and will build defences against experiencing everyday thoughts and feelings which are too distressing to contemplate. These destructive emotions become acted out in the external world of the individual who feels the world is an enemy and has to be approached with great suspicion.

With this poverty goes a feeling of inadequacy and emptiness which is highlighted when this state of mind comes into proximity with another person who is perceived, or may have, a fuller and more enriched personality. Here, envy takes on a central role in dysfunctional human relations. So as to objectively highlight aspects of this state of mind, I have listed in Table 1 items taken from Hobson, Patrick, and Valentine's (1998) personal relatedness profile, which specifically addresses paranoid-schizoid functioning. I shall offer a profile of this state of mind as it manifests in people with severe mental illness. The reader is directed to the work of Hanna Segal (1981, 1986) for a comprehensive overview of these processes, particularly as they present themselves in the formality of a psychoanalytic setting.

Using the first category of Hobson, Patrick, and Valentine's (1998) scale, we can find many of the features of people with severe mental illness. In particular, as stated above, these patients often live with a deep impoverishment which of course, in reality, is true, as they have a mental illness but those who look after them do not. As such, all the arrangements for destructive envy are established and this cannot be underestimated in day-to-day living with these patients.

Staff member A, a bubbly vivacious female in her mid-thirties, had just given birth to her second baby and was announcing to visitors to the unit that she was about to give up working and devote herself full-time to motherhood, all within earshot of a recently admitted, twenty-five-year-old single, female, schizophrenic patient, who had just moved into the unit after a long stay in an acute psychiatric hospital ward. Her demeanour visibly "dropped" on hearing this news from someone without mental illness, who was living a "full life".

The creation of therapeutic atmospheres (which I will talk about in the next chapter) requires staff to be aware of how destructive envious attacks can be inadvertently triggered by insensitive self-disclosures. This can often trigger the other aspects listed in Table 1 in the "Personal relatedness" category, of hostility and revenge, leading to devaluation and idealisation of others. In essence, an impoverished mind is full of negative or bad thoughts and feelings and an internal or external trigger can lead to intense projections of hostility into others, which turns

Table 1. Paranoid-schizoid functioning. Items from personal relatedness profile.

| Scale category | Description |
| --- | --- |
| Personal relatedness | – Vengefulness, retaliation, operating by the "law of talion"<br>– Lack of concern, of people and things<br>– Intense, unvaried, black-or-white exchanges, perhaps wonderful or awful<br>– Clear or subtle indications of locked-in hostility, abuse, victimisation, and/or controlled/controlling relations (including sadomasochism?)<br>– Destructive envy, spoiling, devaluation and/or contempt |
| Characteristics of people ("objects") | – Narcissistic, self-preoccupied, unattuned, using others for self-gratification<br>– Omnipotent, feeling no need of others<br>– Persecutory, untrustworthy, abandoning, deserting<br>– The picture that emerges is of ill-defined, "thin", fragmented and/or amorphous figures |
| Predominant affective states | – Intolerable frustration of sense of deprivation and/or extreme emotional "hunger"<br>– Feelings of claustrophobia and/or intrusion<br>– Flooding anxiety<br>– Uncontrolled rage<br>– Profound empty aloneness |

From Hobson, Patrick, and Valentine (1998).

the recipient of this projection into a "thing" or an inanimate object to be used and abused. All too often in psychiatric settings, these dehumanising processes can leave staff feeling demoralised and bewildered.

In "Characteristics of people" it may be that in descriptions of others, there is really a description of aspects of the self or "internal objects". These are observations of people with severe mental illness that are rarely documented in the traditional psychiatric literature. However, I think this is the heuristic strength of the Kleinian theoretical framework: this particular framework does capture the clinical reality of what happens in mental health settings. Patients are often preoccupied with themselves, with little concern for others. Mental health professionals are left feeling inadequate if no immediate cure is forthcoming.

Patient B relentlessly demanded a cure from his psychiatrist and staff in the unit. If his needs weren't met immediately he would accuse staff of being useless and would make formal complaints as to how bad he was being treated. Concern was met with contempt and he would often threaten staff with the "complaints procedure". Importantly, he had a very poor relationship with his father, whom he felt made him feel "never good enough"

These states of mind are extremely difficult to manage and often staff are left on the defensive and devoid of any compassion. These "help rejecting" or "heart sinking" patients are all too familiar in mental health settings. Again, if staff can be aware of what they are up against, then they will be in a better position to create a therapeutic atmosphere that can best help these patients.

Finally, the "Predominant affective states" as listed in Table 1 are frequently found with people with severe mental illness. The level of emotional neediness found with this particular patient population is huge. On many occasions the demand to fulfil needs immediately is so urgent and intense that professionals are left exhausted, depleted, and drained of any emotional and physical resources. Also, often these patients have a team of professionals who, unwittingly, refill a "bottomless black hole" of neediness with little or no recognition of the effects of containing the negative unwanted parts of these patients, and tolerate the frustration and hostility that comes with this. As such, in Kleinian terms, mental health staff can easily become the "emotional toilet" of the infinite and indefinite needs of patients. Any frustration of immediate gratification is seen as persecution. Lopez-Corvo describes this theory from the work of Wilfred Bion, a post-Kleinian analyst:

> If the capacity to tolerate frustration is adequate the internal "no-breast" will transform into a thought and an apparatus for thinking will be developed, which will make the frustration more bearable. But, if the capacity to deal with frustration is inadequate the internal bad "no-breast" will pressure the mind towards evasion of frustration and instead of forming a thought, the no-breast will transform into a bad object or a Beta-element, indistinguishable from the "thing-in-itself", which will serve only to be evacuated.

> In this case, instead of having an apparatus for thinking, the mind
> will be dominated by mechanisms of projective identification, used
> to discharge the accumulation of bad objects (or acting out). (2003,
> pp. 282–283)

I will describe the concept of projective identification later in this chapter. In respect of this extreme emotional neediness, there often appears this incessant demand for needs to be met now.

Patient C is a fifty-five-year-old man suffering from episodes of severe depression. He would manage the quiet opportunities given to him to speak about what was on his mind with both feelings of emptiness and demands on me to "fill the silence" or "come up with some answers" to his depressive episodes. Any frustration of these demands were felt as bad, rather than an opportunity for him to think about and put words to his thoughts and feelings.

These impoverished but highly charged states of mind also feel intense rage at any deprivation of needs. Often it is difficult, if not impossible, for the worker to "hold the moment" and allow thoughts to emerge. As listed in Table 1, intense anxiety and emotional "rawness" are part of this state of mind, along with a profound sense of being alone and cut off from human relationships.

## Depressive position

This state of mind is the opposite of the paranoid-schizoid position. Unfortunately, for all of us working within the mental health field, it is rarely experienced in day-to-day work with people with severe mental health illness. Thus, the pressure on the professional is enormous, not to be pulled into more negative states of mind or relationships with patients, but to hold on to some semblance of a style of thinking and relating that values thought and concern for the patient. Eric Brenman, an eminent Kleinian psychoanalyst, comments on this pressure within the formality of the consulting room:

> Possibly the most challenging of all narcissistic problems for the
> analyst is the state of affairs where the analyst is made to feel mean-
> ingless and his belief in analysis a futile delusion. How the analyst
> copes with this is of the utmost importance, if he cannot face this
> and differentiate the good and worthwhile from the un-worthwhile,

Table 2. Depressive position functioning. Items from personal relatedness profile.

| State category | Description |
| --- | --- |
| Personal relatedness | – Mutuality allowing freedom for (and potentially loving links between) participants<br>– Participants are able to benefit from the capacities and contributions of others<br>– Genuine, appropriate concern between participants<br>– A capacity for ambivalence, in which the participants struggle with the complexities of relationships<br>– The potential for forgiveness, with a tendency to seek resolution of difficulties and reparation of harm done |
| Characteristics of people ("objects") | – Loyal, committed, "straight"<br>– Emotionally available and caring with recognition of the needs and wishes of others<br>– Able to acknowledge dependence and helplessness without overwhelming anxiety, possibly genuinely grateful<br>– Benign, benevolent, helpful to development<br>– The picture that emerges of three dimensional, substantial, coherent, defined and integrated people |
| Predominant affective states | – Integrated feelings of loss and mourning<br>– The experience of solitude as at times rewarding and beneficial<br>– Overwhelming depression<br>– Feeling gratified, enriched, satisfied, or nourished<br>– Pleasure in sustained closeness and/or intimacy |

he does not meet the depressive position himself and, therefore, cannot give the patient a sufficiently strengthening introject to help the patient meet the depressive position. As you will know, there are patients who are exceptionally skilful in producing this state of mind in the analyst and who attempt to make us act out by reassurance, psychological and physical. They may force the analyst to feel despair—the analyst may act out his experience of rejection by writing the patient off, or adopt an over-rigid position, which blocks fresh experience. (2006, p. 5)

So how does this transfer to the real world of looking after people with severe mental illness in health and social care? Let me describe a typical atmosphere in a psychiatric unit ...

It's the afternoon ward round on a Monday. Patients have come back from weekend passes. A new "first episode" manic depressive patient has been admitted. She believes God has sent her to earth to rid her family of demons. Several staff have phoned in sick. The anorexic patient on the ward continues to refuse to eat. Two aggressive male patients, heavily dosed with anti-psychotic medication, look menacingly at the clinical psychologist who comes to run his weekly group. In the previous week, one patient went AWOL (absent without leave) and had committed suicide.

Maintaining any depressive position functioning in this typical ward atmosphere is indeed a herculean task. So taking into account the descriptions in Table 2, how can we try to create a more "depressive functioning" atmosphere? I will use Table 2 to suggest changes to the ward atmosphere I have just described, to illustrate how this theoretical framework can be applied to everyday psychiatric settings.

The first day of the week (Monday) marks the end of the weekend and the return of, potentially, a full staff team and ward. In taking into consideration the attribute of being "emotionally available and caring with the recognition and wishes of others", the staff could be aware and available to the feelings of patients who remained on the ward over the weekend, feelings of being abandoned while staff were away enjoying their non-mentally ill life. Severe mental illness strips the individual of full engagement with life and living. Often patients will never marry or have partnerships and rarely will they have children. If they do, families will often be torn apart with the destructive effects of their illness. An awareness of "what Monday means" on a ward could make a huge difference to the level of understanding given to patients. The significance of weekend breaks is well recognised in the psychoanalytic literature. Embedding this "loss" for the patient and helping him to explore the meaning of what could have been or might have been is an important feature of a "mini-mourning" process (Steiner, 2012) that lets the patient know that he is understood and we are sensitive to the impact of mental illness.

A new "manic depressive" patient is admitted after the weekend. As in Table 2, could staff demonstrate some genuine appropriate concern for this patient? The subjective experience of mental illness is truly terrifying and all too often we fail to recognise the impact this has on the patient, particularly on a first presentation. This does not mean over-identifying with the patient. Rather, it means taking seriously the fall-out from such a life changing diagnosis. Patients who suffer from severe mental illness have their life changed forever. Putting words to this can facilitate depressive position functioning in the ward atmosphere. To establish this, it is important not to get caught up in the "manic/magical" thinking of the manic depressive. As Brenman suggests, reacting prematurely and quickly to a powerful state of mind prevents a fresh experience or new thinking, which could help alleviate the genuine distress of the patient.

A hospital ward atmosphere is characterised by staff absences which may be because of illness or annual leave. However, rather than ignore the impact of this, it may be helpful to acknowledge that dependencies do exist and have been broken. As listed under "Characteristics of people", to recognise the dependency needs of patients on staff and the ensuing helplessness when this fails can create a more honest and full atmosphere, where patients' disappointments are acknowledged, rather than ignored and their significance devalued.

The clinical psychologist running his weekly group is immediately met with feelings of intimidation rather than intimacy. Hardly the best ingredients for depressive position functioning. So this atmosphere will also suffer from a lack of any meaningful human contact, characteristic of the depressive position. The pressure will be on this clinical psychologist to recognise the internal psychic violence that gives rise to the external physical violence (Kapur, 2005), so as to appreciate the emotional pressures these young men have been under with the life shattering diagnosis of psychosis. Their maleness has been corrupted by the most devastating medical diagnoses which potentially have taken their capacity for potency, fulfilment, and a full life away from them.

Finally, and arguably causing the most devastating impact on the ward atmosphere, has been a loss of life—the patient who has taken his own life. In a depressive position atmosphere this would have involved considerable work and exploration of the meaning of this loss. Feelings of inadequacy, helplessness, and hopelessness would have to be recognised and worked through. The experience of "not being able to reach" (Joseph, 1975) the inner world of this patient would have to be acknowledged as well as the sense of failure of losing someone in this way. For staff, this eats at the very core of what has unconsciously motivated us to go into the helping profession, the repairing of damage done in our psychic or real lives (Klein, 1959).

What I have tried to do so far in this chapter is outline the key features of two states of mind that I think powerfully capture good and bad human relations. In Kleinian theory, it is accepted that a two way arrow exists between these states of mind, often signified by PS ↔ D. The quality of the internal and external worlds of all of us dictates how we are able to remain in the depressive position and recover from the more dysfunctional paranoid-schizoid position. I will describe later in this text the processes to put in place to maximise depressive position functioning. I will now describe other key theoretical ideas to capture important clinical/emotional processes.

## Projection, projective identification and containment

To describe these particular ideas, I will refer to an article I published early in my career, highlighting projective processes in psychiatric settings (Kapur, 1991). I have taken an everyday incident in this setting and will analyse it using the above concepts.

> I walked past the cashier's office where patients wait for their money, on the way to persecute a colleague for failing to keep an appointment to play squash with me the day before. As I turned the corner, I saw a dishevelled, impoverished old man, dressed like a tramp. He held a piece of paper in his hand. He looked agitated and upset and was watching the window of the office with urgency and hope that something would happen. As I passed him, he looked up, muttering to himself. He glimpsed me and then spat out, "Have you got the time?" in an aggressive and intense way. I knew I was in trouble, I was carrying a newspaper in my hand, the *Independent* and I thought I had momentarily become the depriving bad breast. He spat out again, "I want to know the time" and shook his fist

at me. In a flash, momentarily, I felt agitated, upset, angry, as if something had been shot at me.

I knew that if I paused to look down at my watch the delay in replying would be experienced as frustration and persecution would follow. If I told a lie and guessed the time he could rightly accuse me of being dishonest. I looked down at my watch, shaped my mouth to speak and he yelled at me, his fist waving, "I just want to know the fucking time, don't you know anything!" I momentarily wanted to return his projection with professional superiority and tell him he was the patient and I was "staff". I would get the nurses to sort him out. He continued to wave his arms about and I left, having uttered nothing. I turned the corner and heard him yell how awful I was and everyone was. I walked away with a cautious glance behind my shoulder and sighed with relief as I passed through the doors away from this "deprived infant". It was over in thirty seconds! (pp. 36–37)

The location or putting feelings and thoughts about oneself onto others (projection) as well as into others (projective identification) constitutes the backbone of this particular conceptual model of understanding human relations, particularly between a patient and a helper, whether that is a nurse, doctor, clinical psychologist, social worker, psychotherapist, or psychoanalyst. It is how these emotional processes are "contained" that determines how the patient can move from the paranoid-schizoid position to the depressive position.

It was Melanie Klein who gave birth to the concept of projective identification. She first coined the phrase in her seminal paper on "Notes on Some Schizoid Mechanisms" Klein (1946), where she noticed a particular form of identification which establishes the prototype of an aggressive object-relation (p. 8). She described the hatred and wish to harm the other object, mother or breast, which occurs at this turbulent moment. Hostile and negative feelings are "split off and put into others". It becomes a ridding of the self of unwanted aspects which are unbearable to contain. Whatever feels good inside has to be protected by the evacuation of the bad.

It was the post-Kleinian analyst, Wilfred Bion, who used the phrase "containment" to capture how negative feelings and thoughts could be detoxified (alpha processing of raw emotions or what he called beta elements). He, like Klein, suggested the fundamental relationship between baby and the mother's breast creates the blueprint for future human relations.

> It is at the breast where "the infant suffers pangs of hunger and fear that it is dying, wrecked by guilt and anxiety, and impelled by greed, messes itself and cries. The mother picks it up, feeds it and comforts it and eventually the infant sleeps. (1957, p. 31)

A manic-depressive patient, who I worked with for nearly eight years, describes succinctly what containment by me of her meant: "It is at times of my uncontrollable distress, when I most need you, when I need you to stay steady, not take fright, not turn everything upside down, not abandon me, send me shocked, spiralling, plummeting into a world of darkness and despair. If it is too much to ask of you, I understand ... if I am too much."

Returning to the example from the psychiatric setting, hundreds, if not thousands of those moments occur every day within psychiatric environments. However, if they are not contained appropriately, they can lead to an exponential growth of explosive moments which inevitably result in relationships between patients and staff breaking down. Let us analyse the example using the aforementioned concepts of projection, projective identification, and containment.

The incident happened "in a flash": the frustration of feeding experienced by the patient, represented by the closed-down window of the cashier's office and the arrival of a fuller object (me), fuelled an already ignited envy and led to the evacuation of raw feelings (beta elements) where I felt something nasty had been left within me. At that moment I became the "thing-in-itself", a harsh and cruel controlling object. The envy of being side by side with a fellow object was unbearable and an envious attack ensued. The *Independent* represented the state of mind the patient most wanted, yet most hated, because he was without it.

You can gather from this analysis that envy has a central role in this explanatory framework. It is the trigger for aggressive and hostile feelings with the aim of creating a psychic equilibrium by spoiling the hated object. Unfortunately, this represents only a short-lived relief for the deprived and envious object, as the impoverished feelings soon return.

The role of envy cannot be underestimated in understanding psychopathology, particularly in the interface between the mentally ill patient and the mental health professional. Attention to this in creating a therapeutic atmosphere is crucial for the patient to feel contained and understood. Let me say a bit more about this with particular reference to Melanie Klein's classic (1957) paper on "Envy and Gratitude". In the psychoanalytic consulting room, she observes:

> The analyst has just given an interpretation which has brought the patient relief and produced a change of mood from despair to hope. With some patients, or with the same patient at other times, this helpful interpretation may soon become the object of destructive criticism. It is then no longer felt to be something good he has received and has experienced as enrichment. His criticism may attach itself to minor points, the interpretation should have been given earlier, it was too long and has disturbed the patient's associations; or it was too short and this implies that he has not been sufficiently understood. The envious patient grudges the analyst the success of his work; and if he feels that the analyst and the help he is giving have become spoilt and devalued by his envious criticism, he cannot introject sufficiently as a good object nor accept his interpretations with real conviction and assimilate them. Real conviction, as we often see in less envious patients implies gratitude for a gift received. (pp. 183–184)

So, transfer this to the everyday moment I described earlier or other interactions where something good is being genuinely given to the patient, whether that is a concerned psychiatrist offering the right medication, a social worker offering social support, a psychiatric nurse being concerned about the mental state of the patient, or a clinical psychologist putting together a well thought-out intervention.

If the mental health worker can be aware that "good can trigger bad" then not only is there more hope for the patient that good things can be held on to and retrieved, but also staff may feel less demoralised and prone to give up or "refer on" when their well intentioned efforts break down.

## Transference and countertransference

Perhaps the two most powerful concepts in psychoanalytic theory can be best captured with the power of the transference in making an emotional reality (phantasy) where we often appear to others not as we are, but as a constellation of past experiences, particularly when we are in the role of any authority; and similarly, countertransference can be described as at times having thoughts and feelings that don't really belong to us, but other people who may be putting parts of themselves onto (projection) and into (projective identification) us.

The predominant use of these ideas in the formality of a psycho-analytic setting has deprived mental health professionals of valuable insights into helping patients with severe mental illness. If we return to the description of the incident in the psychiatric hospital, we can see that in the transference I was:

- An enriched, full, and "bountiful" object (person).
- A depriving object (person).

In the countertransference I felt:

- Idealised.
- Withholding.
- Superior.
- Upset.
- Threatened.

So, if I put this understanding together, I could have an insight into the internal world of the patient (impoverished and full of rage) and its effect on me (pressurised, agitated, and tense). Maybe with this increased understanding I could, as Brenman (2006) suggests, regain some depressive functioning and react in a thoughtful way, rather than "acting out the countertransference" through persecuting this clearly damaged state of mind.

## Psychotic and non-psychotic personalities

I am indebted here to two supervisors at the Willesden Centre for Psychological Treatment in London (Ms. Jocelyn Richards and Dr. Michael Sinason) for their supervision and teaching in this powerful idea of helping me understand severe mental illness and destructive emotional processes with disturbed states of mind (Sinason, 1993). It was Wilfred Bion, a post-Kleinian psychoanalyst, who first developed the concept of psychotic and non-psychotic personalities to understand the clinical phenomena encountered in the psychoanalytic consulting room. I will use Sinason's description to summarise Bion's concept:

> Bion has described how the difficulty of dealing with psychic pain can give rise to the development of two parts of the personality. Each with a very different way of coping. The psychotic part, intolerant of frustration, gets rid of its perceptions and the part of the mind that registers them. The non-psychotic part of the personality which retains a capacity for tolerating psychic pain is able to experience jealousy or envy or disappointment without denying the experience and without attempting to change his attitude to the object in order to avoid these experiences. (1993, pp. 209–210)

Clinically, this would manifest itself in the following account from a patient in individual psychoanalytic psychotherapy: "It's as if there are two me's. A me that wants a better life but another me that feels I am so bad and ugly I don't deserve any good things. And that me hates other people's ordinary happy life. It's only by living near the edge that I can feel good, but that just burns me out. The other me can feel like a spectator watching me destroy things around me."

I think this very powerful clinical understanding is essential when working with people with severe mental illness. Often these patients are out of control and need the sanity of the psychiatric system to keep them safe. In its most powerful form, the psychotic personality or "mad self" feels both omnipotent and arrogant and needs the "brick mother" of the asylum to keep it safe. When this is done, there may then be an opportunity to link in with the non-psychotic or "sane self" that is interested in progress and recovery. However, the grip of the psychotic personality or "mad self" cannot be overestimated. Sinason (1993) uses an excerpt from C. S. Lewis's book, *The Great Divorce* to highlight the struggle between the sane or non-psychotic personality (the Angel), the patient (the Ghost), and the "mad" or psychotic personality (the Lizard):

> I saw coming towards us a Ghost who carried something on his shoulder. Like all the Ghosts, he was unsubstantial, but they differed from one another as smokes differ. Some had been whitish, this one was dark and oily. What sat on his shoulder was a little

red lizard and it was twitching its tail like a whip and whispering things in his ear. As we caught sight of him he turned his head to the reptile with a snarl of impatience. "Shut up, I tell you" he said. It wagged its tail and continued to whisper to him. He ceased snarling and presently began to smile. Then he turned and started to limp westward, away from the mountains.

"Off so soon?" said a voice.

The speaker was more or less human in shape but larger than a man and so bright that I could hardly look at him. His presence smote on my eyes and on my body too (for there was heat coming from him as well as light) like the morning sun at the beginning of a tyrannous summer day.

"Yes, I'm off" said the Ghost. "Thanks for all your hospitality. But it's no good you see, I told this little chap" (here he indicated the lizard) "that he'd have to be quiet if he came—which he insisted on doing. Of course his stuff won't do here, I realise that. But he won't stop. I shall just have to go home."

"Would you like me to make him quiet?" said the flaming Spirit—an Angel, as I now understood.

"Of course I would" said the Ghost.

"Then I will kill him" said the Angel, taking a step forward.

"Oh, ah, look out. You're burning me. Keep away" said the Ghost, retreating.

"Don't you want him killed?"

"You didn't say anything about killing him at first. I hardly meant to bother you with anything so drastic as that."

"It's the only way" said the Angel, whose burning hands were now very close to the lizard. "Shall I kill it?"

"Well, that's a further question. I'm quite open to consider it but it's a new point, isn't it? I mean, for the moment I was only thinking about silencing it because up here—well, it's so damned embarrassing."

"May I kill it?"

"Well, there's time to discuss that later."

"There is no time. May I kill it?"

The key idea from this piece is how the lizard not only has a powerful grip on the Ghost or patient, but how the Ghost is terrified at losing all identity if the lizard is killed off by the Angel. Sinason makes the crucial clinical point that we have to respect the integrity and identity of the Ghost/lizard arrangement and then offer an alternative which offers hope of a different and "saner" emotional life. He writes of the importance of recognising how the psychotic personality, or mad self, can get the analyst to work outside the understanding, non-persecutory, and containing analytic frame to persecute or reject the patient.

> The treatment approach puts analytic researchers at the centre of the enterprise and the analyst will not be drawn out of the analytic frame in any way. All actions are abrogated and resistance to free association examined carefully, since it is usually mediated by the patient being fed paranoid propaganda by his cohabiter (the lizard in the C. S. Lewis excerpt). He is advised by his cohabiter of the dangerous outcomes of letting the analyst know of matters that he would prefer to keep in the dark ... (An) unexpected finding is that the cohabitee can experience hurt if the therapist actually uses the very value-laden denigratory or criticising terms which one promulgated and invited by the cohabitee. (p. 219)

I think his last point is crucial for mental health workers who can find themselves rejecting or persecuting patients with severe mental illness. To create a therapeutic atmosphere it is essential to take seriously the strength and silent nature of the "lizard's" influence on the patient's destructive behaviour. While not abrogating responsibility, it is essential as Sinason suggests to see the patient with two minds. Often "help rejecting" or "heart sinking" patients will "pick a fight" to act out the phantasies of the mad self, so confirming their own harsh and negative view of themselves and then "biting the hand that feeds them" with the mental health worker failing to contain and understand the nature of this powerful, hidden, emotional force.

### Destructive narcissism, narcissistic identificate, attacks on linking, and internal saboteur

I will consider these four powerful concepts together as they have one outcome in common, a destruction of good and healthy internal and external object relations. As a patient recently said to me: "There is something powerful that has been chronically resident in my mind as long as I can remember. It hates me feeling good and joyful about myself and other people, yet it makes me feel good because it gets its excitement out of putting other people down. I can't live without it, yet I know it leaves me and other people feeling miserable."

Another concept used to capture this clinical phenomenon is the negative therapeutic reaction. Grotstein (1979) describes this occurrence in the formality of a psychoanalytic consulting room:

> When one aspect of the patient would make successful contact with the analyst and approach "salvation", another portion of the personality—seemingly a more helpless one which was experienced as already being too badly off and too incurable and too unanalysed—would enviously attack its more successful rival and seek to undermine its relationship to the analyst. It would also remind the patient of that pact he or she had made to purchase his safety in a bygone time as well as remind the patient that his attempt for salvation is futile. (p. 413)

This, of course, is similar to the "voice of the lizard" in the C. S. Lewis story and can inform the mental health professional that their goodness may be enviously attacked and devoured, which unfortunately becomes a state of overexcitement for the patient that fuels their psychopathology.

It is overexcitement that is at the core of the idea of destructive narcissism. Herbert Rosenfeld (1971a) drew attention to this particular idea when he wrote:

> There are some narcissistic patients where defused destructive impulses seem to be constantly active and dominate the whole of their personality and object relations. They express their feelings in an only slightly disguised way by devaluing the analyst's work with their persistent indifference, sickly repetitive behaviour and sometimes open belittlement. In this way they assert their superiority over the analyst, representing life and creativity by wasting or destroying his work, understanding and satisfaction. They feel superior in being able to control and withhold parts of themselves which want to depend on the analyst as a helpful person. (p. 248)

He goes on to describe the internal world of the patient in an often cited piece of his work which is helpful in letting the other person, whether that is the analyst or helping professional, "know what they are up against".

> The destructive narcissism of these patients appears often highly organised, as if one were dealing with a powerful gang dominated by a leader, who controls all of the members of the gang to see they support one another in making the criminal destructive work more effective and powerful. However, the narcissistic organisation not only measures the strength of the destructive narcissism, but it has a defensive purpose, to keep itself in power and so maintain the "status quo". The main aim seems to be to prevent the weakening of the organisation and to control the members of the gang so that they will not desert the destructive organisation and join the positive parts of the self or betray the secrets of the gang to the Police, the protecting superego, standing for the helpful analyst who might be able to save the patient. (ibid., p. 249)

My contention is that we as mental health professionals see so much destructive narcissism in our everyday work with patients with severe mental illness. Perhaps as Rosenfeld suggests, in the analytic setting we not only know what we are up against, but we also know that patients will have negative reactions to both "being given too much too soon" and signs of helpful progress. The destructive processes are part and parcel of Bion's "psychotic personality" and if we take seriously that this is qualitatively and quantitatively greater in psychotic rather than neurotic patients, then we are up against powerful forces dedicated to "getting their kicks" out of seeing themselves and others destroyed. For the mental health professional the task, a huge one, is how to maintain good and helpful progress in the face of violent opposition to progress.

In the minutiae of analytic work, Steiner (1993), and more recently in 2012, has described the vulnerability the patient feels if he emerges from this psychic safety or what he calls "retreat". While this may rarely be captured in day-to-day work in mental health, I think this idea is useful to describe patients who "live in a world of their own". Using one particular theoretical understanding, we can see that it is indeed a complex internal world with complex processes all designed to oppose positive changes and most of all, depending on someone else for help.

Steiner (2012) writes:

> The patient who has hidden himself in the retreat often dreads emerging from it because it exposes him to anxieties and suffering—which is often precisely what had led him to deploy the defences

in the first place. However, the first and the most immediate consequence of emerging from a psychic retreat is a feeling of being exposed and observed. It is here that feelings of embarrassment, shame and humiliation commonly occur. (p. 3)

For patients with severe mental illness, this vulnerability is huge and the external world is judged to be hostile and rejecting with the inevitability that they remain in their psychic retreat. Perhaps if mental health staff were aware of this state of mind they could provide an atmosphere whereby some emergence from this psychic retreat is possible and thus the patient feels less withdrawn and left alone with huge anxieties.

In focusing more closely on the internal world of a narcissistic state of mind, the analyst Leslie Sohn coined the phrase "narcissistic identificate" to capture the strength of an object that is controlling how a severely mentally ill patient relates to himself and others. In his seminal paper in 1985 he writes:

To me it appears that in the narcissistic organisation, an identification by projective identification has taken place; the process of identification starts the narcissistic organisation; that is to say, by becoming the object, which is then felt to be within possession of the self.

It is this that produces the feeling which we call omnipotence, or which enhances the intrinsic omnipotence that is present in all of us and accounts for the strong bland arrogance of these patients, who can then think, do, be and exert all the influences of the original object. It has all the chameleonic satisfaction of being a new object and wishes to stay that way. It is, however, done destructively and can never be used constructively—the destruction being to the state of the ego and to the object which is consequently devalued. This accounts for the hollowness of such a process, which so differentiates it from normal identification. (pp. 277–278)

While this is a difficult concept to grasp, I think it is helpful in accepting the enormity of the destructive forces opposing the mental health worker who is failing such a patient. What Sohn helps us with is understanding how the severely mentally ill patient holds within his mind an identification with fake and damaged parts of the self and others, which opposes and hates dependency upon others. This "character in itself" feels smug and superior, yet remains isolated and aloof from others, all the time giving the appearance of engaging with others. For example, a severely mentally ill patient once said to me about my enquiry as to whether he was improving in one of our projects: "You collect all this information but you don't really give a damn. You just sit there in your big office pretending you care. You can never help me."

Not only is this patient adopting an aloofness but he is also internally identifying with a superior self who projects into me an "uncaring self". The latter in fact represents his own view of himself with his "caring self" nowhere to be seen. For me, it felt like I was running a factory production line, rather than a therapeutic milieu for severely mentally ill patients.

I will now describe an important phenomenon captured by Bion (1959) which impedes any positive gains in working with mentally ill patients. "Attacks on linking" was a phrase used to describe how patients with a state of mind predominated by sadism, destructive impulses, and hate, with a mercurial relationship with the analyst, literally "deadens" their connection to ongoing work. In essence, the goodness offered by an analyst can all feel too much and the envious "psychotic" personality within the patient can only destroy the hand that feeds it and is unable to take in the good experience. He writes:

> Observation of the patient's disposition to attack the link between two objects is simplified because the analyst has to establish a link with the patient and does this by verbal communication and his equipment of psychoanalytical experience. Upon this the creative relationship depends and, therefore, we should be able to see attacks being made upon it. (p. 88)

For the purposes of this text the key issues, as with the other concepts reviewed in this chapter, are that if the mental health worker offers a good and substantial experience (with some qualities that Bion refers to as the "psychoanalytical experience of concern and a deep understanding of the patient") there is a likelihood that this will be attacked. So many times in everyday interactions in psychiatry, I have witnessed the "good" offered by well-meaning staff attacked and devalued by severely mentally ill patients, with the result being demoralisation and the regression to persecutory behaviour from the helping professional. Perhaps keeping in mind that this phenomenon occurs outside the consulting room will help the professional understand the intensity of attacks on her good work.

Finally, I will describe Fairbairn's concept of an "internal saboteur" to capture the three dimensional nature of pathological internal object relations that can occur with severely mentally ill states of mind. Fairbairn (1994), like Melanie Klein, suggested that the crucial relationship between the mother and baby dictates the future emotional/ psychic growth of the individual. Either the baby can attach himself to the healthy or usual ego of the mother, or he can become split off into two repressed internal object relationships. This is either to a libidinal ego attached to an exciting object or an anti-libidinal ego attached to a rejecting self, the internal saboteur, or a negative object. These four internal objects are identified with an unloving mother in her exciting and rejecting qualities, particularly when a healthy or loving mother is absent. What is of relevance to understanding the state of mind of someone with severe mental illness, is that there is a complex interplay of these internal object relationships that can become acted out in the transference. Ogden (2010) describes this inner world as follows:

> The relationship between the internal saboteur and the rejecting object derives from the infant's love of his mother despite (and because of) her rejection of him. The nature of the pathological love that binds together the internal saboteur and the rejecting object is a bond not of hate, but of a pathological love that is experienced as bitter "resentment". Neither the rejecting object nor the internal saboteur is willing or able to think about, much less relinquish, that tie. In fact, there is no desire on the part of either to change anything about their mutual dependence. The power of that bond is impossible to over-estimate. (p. 111)

How does this manifest itself in the relationship with others in the external world? I think we can witness two things with this state of mind. First, the internal object relationships are so powerful and in a "trance" with each other, that others are "locked out" of any relatedness with the patient. This is not unlike Rosenfeld's description of the "internal mafia gang". Second, others will be rejected and their best efforts will be sabotaged in trying to make any helpful relationships with this state of mind. Clinically, I have found this often where one patient's view is: "I will undermine your best efforts to help me and reject it at any opportunity." The parallel internal subjective state is: "I hate myself and accept nothing good about myself. Any good I do, I will spoil because I feel I am nothing."

So, for the helper, any effort to relate requires a full understanding of how s/he could be repelled and undermined while at the same time keeping in mind there is a "healthy central ego" that is interested in ordinary help and human warmth.

### *Interpretation—putting into words*
### *"who is doing what to whom"*

How we speak to the patient is crucial in deciding how we are approaching the patient's state of mind and the request to alleviate and improve his level of distress. Common styles in the psychological therapies range from questioning, clarification, informing, suggesting, and confronting to interpretation. Clara Hill, a researcher in counselling psychology, has devised a taxonomy of interventions (1978) which I think captures the wide range of speaking styles. One of these is interpretation, but her definition is not based in the particular theoretical framework described in this text. For this approach I will use a definition based on this approach, which formed the basis of my doctoral research and subsequently has been used in post-doctoral research (Hobson & Kapur, 2005). This definition is: "… a comment by the therapist to the individual which is directed towards bringing to the surface meanings of the communication that has occurred. An interpretation is an hypothesis by the therapist of the meaning of the utterance."

The definition goes on to rate as high, comments that make a specific reference to the relationship between the therapist or analyst and patient, and rate as low, those comments that do not. The findings from my doctoral research (Kapur, 1998) as they apply to working with severely mentally ill patients will be reported in Chapter Six of this book.

I will not review the literature of interpretation in this chapter or the book. Rather, it will suffice to say that the above definition has been distilled from the theoretical framework outlined above. Of particular interest in this approach is a "containing" interpretation that draws attention to the relationship between helper and patient. Paula Heimann (1956), writing on transference interpretation, points to the technique of putting words of "who is doing what to whom". Here it is

important for the mental health professional not to be overwhelmed by
the mystery of this technique or to be taken over by an idea that formal
psychoanalytic procedures are being invoked in the ideas of this text.
Rather, the essence of this text is that people with severe mental illness
may find it helpful to have those working with them understand better
the processes that are taking place in their exchanges and perhaps ena-
ble the patients to put into words how they are relating to themselves
and others—particularly in relation to the helper. Many examples will
be given as to how this can work in individual, group, and other settings but typical comments are as follows:

> "When you first come into the project you must have felt worried
> about who you were going to meet, how you were going to be
> accepted by others, particularly me, as your keyworker. Meeting
> strangers for the first time is always difficult."
>
> "When I gave you the medication after you were upset, I think
> you felt I was forcing you to be quiet, rather than helping you to
> calm down."
>
> "After my annual leave you didn't seem to want to speak to me.
> Maybe you were making me feel what you felt when I cut myself
> off, silenced myself, by going on leave?"
>
> "When you came into the project there was a 'you' that felt
> accepted and understood. However, this all seemed to become too
> much and it was as if another 'you' took over and destroyed things
> here by your constant devaluation of staff and provocation of oth-
> ers to reject and persecute you."

The key idea is that by capturing the state of mind of the severely mentally ill patient in an ordered, structured, and thoughtful atmosphere,
he will feel his state of mind is being taken seriously with the hope that
he will experience some easement of his difficulties and distress that
may help to improve his overall functioning and move him to a better
state of mind.

# CHAPTER TWO

# Therapeutic communities, environments, and atmospheres

The predominant movement in the UK, Europe, and the United States has been to focus on the therapeutic community idea as the only model to maximise the therapeutic aspects of psychiatric settings. I will briefly review the therapeutic community movement and key principles as well as outlining the rather contemporary idea of a therapeutic environment. Having done this, I will propose a new idea, "therapeutic atmospheres", which I believe can be created in most psychiatric, mental health, and social care settings and which, I think, create the best opportunity for the patient to make a personal, clinical, and social recovery from severe mental illness.

## Therapeutic communities

One of the pioneers of the therapeutic community movement, Maxwell Jones, outlines what he sees as the key elements of this idea:

> But the creation of a therapeutic community calls for the learning of a particularly immediate and personal kind on the part of all involved. To some extent this takes place in a day-to-day fashion, but particular crises in the community offer opportunities for

intensified learning, or what we call living-learning experiences. These involve face-to-face confrontation of all the people concerned and the joint analysis of the current interpersonal difficulty. Each individual is helped to become more aware of the thinking and feelings of the others and this leads to a more comprehensive and holistic view of the situation as it affects each of the people involved. (1968, p. 106)

The emphasis in the early and contemporary therapeutic community movements (Campling, Davies, & Farquharson, 2004) is still very much on these interpersonal aspects of group or community processes. These initial ideas became crystallised in Rappaport's (1960) four principles of a therapeutic community:

- Democratisation, where each member of the community shares equality in the exercise of power and decision about community matters.
- Permissiveness, where all members are encouraged to tolerate each other with behaviours which are deemed "extraordinary", such as hostile or rejecting behaviour.
- Communalism, where there is a personal rapport and sense of belonging between everyone in the community.
- Reality confrontation, which refers to the process identified by Maxwell Jones above, where the view is that residents should be confronted with the views of others to offer a more accurate picture of their effects on themselves and others.

In the contemporary therapeutic community movement, these principles are similar to the values and style of group analysis. The therapeutic community movement is led by this therapeutic model (Haigh, 2007; Kennard, 2008) and forms the national "Community of Communities" accreditation body. This body peer reviews and oversees therapeutic community projects in the UK, of which Threshold is a part (www.repsych.ac.uk/cru/communityofcommunities.htm). So as to highlight the key elements of a therapeutic community environment, I will list and then discuss the main factors captured in their peer review. I will comment on the theoretical basis behind these factors as linked to the contemporary psychoanalytic movement and then later in this chapter note the similarities and differences to my idea of a "therapeutic atmosphere".

## Community processes

In this factor there is an emphasis on how leadership functions in a way that is consistent with a therapeutic community's core values of communalism, democratisation, permissiveness, and reality confrontation. Residents are involved in the day-to-day running of the community and they are aware of the expectations of community membership. Community members are encouraged to form a relationship with the community and are actively invited to be involved in the emotional life of the community. Both staff and patients are involved in setting and maintaining community boundaries and are involved in actions when boundaries are broken. Within the therapeutic community there are structured opportunities for enjoyment in individual work, small groups, and the weekly community meeting. All behaviour and emotional expression is open to discussion, where residents and staff are encouraged and supported to put thoughts and feelings into words. Everything that happens in the community is treated as a learning opportunity where formal individual and group settings are used to explore thoughts and feelings. There is a shared responsibility in the community for the emotional and physical safety of each other. Residents, along with staff, are involved in allocating jobs and responsibilities in the community. Overall, there is an ethos of equal and mutual participation between staff and residents, with a "flattening of hierarchies" culture.

## Staffing

Job descriptions should reflect the needs of the therapeutic community with an expectation that community members are involved in some aspect of selection of new staff members. Competencies are clearly defined for staff working in a therapeutic community. Staff levels are set, and specific training in working in a therapeutic community is provided, to ensure relevant experience is available to ensure the smooth running of a project. Regular staff supervision along with a weekly staff sensitivity group is an important part of the professional infrastructure of a therapeutic community.

## Joining and leaving

There is a planned joining process for prospective community members so that new members are prepared before entering what for them is a new group. Assessment of new residents is well planned in conjunction with the service user. At the end of a member's stay in the community, there is a planned leaving process involving the resident exploring the impact of departure on both the individual and the community.

## Therapeutic framework

The therapeutic programme is overseen by appropriately qualified staff, and is also underpinned by psychodynamic/psychoanalytic theory. Each resident has a plan that highlights personal therapeutic/ educational needs and how they can be met through engagement in the community. Both staff and residents are invited to explore conflicts and issues within the boundaries of the community.

## External relations and performance

The therapeutic community has an active and open approach to external relationships and information is regularly shared with professionals and carers. The community systematically collects data that will help provide evidence for its effectiveness.

We can see that these factors form all structural aspects of the living environment as well as paying attention to links to the external organisational environment and the importance of evaluating outcomes. While most therapeutic communities (including Threshold) meet these standards, each therapeutic community has its own unique and individual emphasis. I shall comment on Threshold's therapeutic atmospheres later in this and subsequent chapters. However, before I do this, I will refer to other models of therapeutic communities that have their own particular style. Kennard (2008) reviews these different styles.

One of the significant models in the therapeutic community movement was linked to the anti-psychiatry movement and the work of R. D. Laing. In this model, there is no such diagnosis as people having a mental illness, and thus staff and patients are seen as equal in this respect. People with psychosis need a "place to be rather than medication and are only asked what they feel able to do" (Berke, 1980). This style of therapeutic community had a "charismatic feel" to it and led to similar developments in Italy (Pedriali, 1997), England (Berke, 1980; Berke, Mascoliner, & Ryan, 1995), and California (Mosher, 2004). The principles incorporated are as follows (taken from Kennard, 2008):

- Treat everyone with dignity and respect.
- Guarantee a quiet, safe, supportive, and protective setting.
- Ensure a "roof over" the patient's head and food.
- Recovery, manifested through maintaining "hope" is expected, without resorting to anti-psychotic drugs.

In summary, to encompass the wide range of therapeutic community movements from the York Retreat (Tuke, 1813) and the original work of Elly Jansen with the Richmond Fellowship (Jansen, 1980), to the embedding of therapeutic community principles from Jones (1964) and Rappaport (1960) and the contemporary conceptualisations by the "Community of Communities", the conclusion reached by Kennard (2008), I think, is most accurate:

> At the risk of over-simplification, we may conclude that this review
> of the history of therapeutic communities for people suffering from
> psychosis has found the following simple yet powerful commodity,
> personal respect and everyday relationships in calm, emotionally
> containing environments. (p. 14)

While I think this is a laudable aspiration by the therapeutic community movement, I do believe it is an outcome that may not be entirely met by this style of work, as it does not fully pay attention to the depth of the psychopathology that staff face in working with severely mentally ill patients and thus key "atmospheric" ingredients are missed. Before I describe what I believe these are (in this and subsequent chapters) I will briefly review the idea of a therapeutic environment.

## Therapeutic environments

The term "therapeutic environment" is a generic term that has been used to apply to a whole range of psychiatric settings where there has been a serious attempt to make people with severe mental illness feel more included and engaged with staff and fellow patients. A contemporary definition similar to what the National Mental Health Unit calls an "enabling environment" (www.enablingenvironments.com) is:

> The psychologically informed environment (PIE) can be created in a
> service such as a hostel or day centre where the social environment

makes people feel emotionally safe ... This includes trying to understand people's behaviour, helping them to be involved with others in a genuine way and to take as much responsibility for themselves as possible. (National Mental Health Unit, 2010, p. 19)

Davies and Abbot (2007) describe such environments as making a conscious attempt to offer a highly supportive environment with the emphasis on relationships within the context of a relaxed non-restrictive approach that maximises the opportunities for "user involvement". This does involve staff in residential psychiatric and mental health settings taking the lead in implementing such ideas as small or large group work to offer focused opportunities for patients to meet with staff in a quiet setting to speak about how they feel about themselves and others. This may take the form of group therapy interventions (e.g., Kapur et al., 1988; Rice & Rutan, 1997; Yalom, 1970) or other similar activities that focus on the individual emotional needs of the patient. The Royal College of Psychiatrists lists the following ten core standards of such an enabling environment as:

1. Belonging, the nature and quality of relationships are of primary importance.
2. Boundaries, there are expectations of behaviour and processes to be maintained and reviewed.
3. Communication, where it is recognised that people communicate in different ways.
4. Development, where there are opportunities to be spontaneous and to try new things.
5. Involvement, where everyone shares responsibility for the environment.
6. Safety, so that support is available for everyone.
7. Structure, so that engagement and purposeful activity is actively encouraged.
8. Empowerment to others, so that power and authority are open to discussion.
9. Leadership, so that responsibility is taken for the environment to be enabling.
10. Openness, where external relationships are sought and valued.

Rudolf Moos has been involved in measuring therapeutic environments for over thirty years (Moos, 1997). His two scales, the Community

Oriented Programs Environment Scale (1996a) and the Ward Atmosphere Scale (1996b) assess the social climate of hospital based psychiatric programmes and residential community programmes, respectively. They are both conceptually similar and are based on staff and patient perceptions of characteristics of the treatment environment. Engagement, independence and order/structure in the daily environment are seen as key therapeutic ingredients for the overall effectiveness of these settings. I will describe these measures and associated findings in the research chapter of this book (Chapter Six).

Overall, I think we can view therapeutic environments as purposeful and activity orientated and aimed at giving patients the best opportunity to express their individuality and ability to relate to others in a well led and structured setting. While there is no explicit framework, this type of setting is of help to patients in their recovery and rehabilitative journey.

## Therapeutic atmospheres

The crucial ingredient in this different approach to working with the severely mentally ill is the use of the term "patient", rather than client, service user, or any other term. The essence of this argument is that a person who suffers from severe mental illness must be:

- Taken seriously as to the depth and breadth of the impairment of his functioning.
- Allowed to have limitations as to what he hopes to achieve in the context of such an illness.
- Able to know that those helping him are not naïve about the significant impairment that takes place.

While this approach may have some hallmarks of the "medical model", it does this within the context of the theoretical framework outlined above. To describe this approach, I will use the familiar concept of Maslow's hierarchy (1954), as represented in Figure 1, to address the emotional needs of people with severe mental illness. I will comment briefly on the "basic, practical, and interactive" ingredients of this approach but will particularly focus on the emotional needs. The crucial aspect of this model is that progression must be from the "bottom up" to ensure that patients feel they are being looked after in a total, comprehensive way. All too often, staff have "gone to the top, forgetting

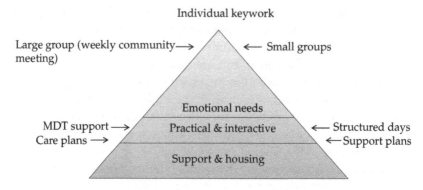

Figure 1. Maslow's hierarchy.

about the bottom" of the hierarchy as this can seem professionally more attractive. However, this invariably means there is no foundation on which to base the emotional work. A prerequisite for emotional work is for the patient to feel safe within a "secure base" (Bowlby, 1988) and from then, in a structured environment, to progress to his emotional needs being met.

## Housing

It was the TAPS (Team for the Assessment of Psychiatric Services) study in the late 1990s (Leff, 1997; Leff & Trieman, 2000; Trieman & Leff, 2002) which indicated that people with severe mental illness have a greater likelihood of achieving better outcomes in the community than if they had stayed in hospital. The findings relevant to this text are that while the social networks remained the same after discharge into a housing environment, the quality of these networks improved. Importantly, the social environment was dramatically less restrictive than a hospital with 84% wanting to stay in their community homes. Finally, the majority of patients did not return to hospital. Locally, in Northern Ireland, these positive findings were replicated (Donnelly et al., 1996) although in both studies there was an increase in mortality rates with more elderly patients.

So, overall, providing a "good homely environment" is associated with better outcomes. Within Threshold, our seven buildings are provided by local housing associations and we receive Housing Benefit funding from our local government body, the Northern Ireland Housing

Executive (www.threshold-services.co.uk). Over two thirds of our running costs are met by the Supporting People programme of funding, to cover staff and other costs for our ninety-two beds. We also have a Floating Support Service for up to thirty patients which is aimed at supporting people with mental health problems to stay in their own homes.

## Care and support plans

Kingdon (1994) outlines the key elements of the above as:

- Assessment of health and social care needs.
- A key worker to co-ordinate care.
- A written care plan.
- A regular review of the plan.
- Inter-professional collaboration.
- Consultation with service users and patients.

I will be using the term care plans to refer to support plans as they are similar, with the latter more accurately describing a plan for someone in a housing/social care environment.

The idea behind these plans is to give the patient an experience of individualised care, tailored to his particular needs, which is often reviewed on a three, six, or twelve monthly basis. Risk assessment and risk management is also embedded into the plan, particularly taking into account that a history of "harm to self and others" inevitably means the patient is at higher risk in any new placement. More recently, the recovery model has highlighted the need for "positive risk taking" to ensure that patients have an opportunity to explore new settings, so reversing the "risk averse" culture that has been a feature of mental health settings (Holloway, 2007).

## Structured days

Good psychiatric care involves the fragmented and disturbed state of mind of the patient being 'held' (Winnicott, 1965) within a structured environment. From the moment they awake to when they go to sleep, all patients should have a structured day that they can become engaged in. While levels of engagement will depend on the motivation of each particular patient, it is important that an "unstructured mind" has a structured day to form the skeleton of the patient's day-to-day living. Also, key workers allocated to patients have a responsibility to monitor engagement and progress with the activities of the day to ensure that when patients lose interest or motivation they are not "forgotten about", and benevolently to follow up those who drop out of any activities.

## Emotional needs

The fundamental difference between the idea of therapeutic atmospheres and the other models described in this chapter is the emphasis placed on the following factors:

## Understanding

In this particular style there is a very clear idea as to the depth of psychopathology facing the worker, both in everyday interactions and also in formal individual and group sessions. I think the depth and breadth of psychopathology has been underestimated in other therapeutic models, thus placing unrealistic expectations on both staff and patients.

Patients with severe mental illness will "inhabit and live in" a complex psychic retreat (Steiner, 1993) where they are very much in a world of their own. Their mad voice inside (Sinason, 1993) or narcissistic identificate (Sohn, 1985) will ensure that they will show little or no interest in relating to others in anything but a superficial way. Their relationships with staff and patients will be dominated by the propaganda of a powerful internal mafia gang (Rosenfeld, 1987) which will oppose all meaningful and helpful human relations. Their world will be the paranoid-schizoid state of mind (Segal, 1981, 1986) and the best efforts of staff to offer a substantial and hopeful emotional experience will be attacked (Bion, 1957). They will be exposed to rejecting and sabotaging relationships (Fairbairn, 1944).

So where has the hope gone? Is my model so pessimistic that we should give up trying to help these patients to emerge into a more purposeful world where there can be some recovery? I think the possibility of personal recovery should have a "contained hope": a hope which the mental health professional has that change is possible within the context of the powerful destructive processes that enviously attack change. All too often, mental health professionals set goals and outcomes that are unrealistic in the context of what they are facing. This leads to disappointment from both the worker and the patient. Assessing the depth and breadth of the emotional state of mind of the patient can mean the worker not only becomes less disillusioned, but also lessens the chance of the patient feeling even more helpless and hopeless when inevitable disappointments occur which are often in the control of the mad self (Sinason, 1993) rather than the sane self who wants to get better.

Winnicott (1963) in his paper, "The Mentally Ill in Your Caseload", gave advice to psychiatric social workers as to how to manage their patients. I will list these recommendations and add my own emphasis:

- "You apply yourself to the case." Whether you be the analyst, therapist, psychiatrist, clinical psychologist, psychiatric social worker or key worker in the patient's life, you do take on an importance in the internal world of the patient. His "sane self" is crying out for some order and meaning to the chaotic world of the paranoid-schizoid position. So each case is important. The patient will "watch your comings and goings" with great interest. Apply yourself to the individuality of the patient and he will be grateful for this.
- "You get to know what it feels like to be your client." Experience the patient within a structured theoretical framework so that the subjective experience of madness can be objectively understood and contained. Not only will this prevent overidentification with the patient, but it will also lessen the chance of the "mad self" of yourself (the mental health professional) colluding with the "mad self" of the patient to arrive at all kinds of ideas to get the patient cured rather then slowly, and carefully, understanding and moving forward with "some" hopes and goals as to what can be achieved. It will also lessen the chance of "help rejecting" or "heart sinking" patients setting the professional up to fail.
- "You become reliable for the limited field of your professional responsibility." For a chaotic and fragmented state of mind, it is essential that the mental health professional "arrives when she says she is going to" and has a clear "start and finish" time. Any chaotic or fragmented relatedness from the mental health professional will only exacerbate the internal world of the patient. Most of all, using terms

like "I'm too busy" or "I've got an urgent appointment elsewhere" will only add to the feelings of inadequacy, hopelessness, and "I'm not worth it" that the patient carries with him. The internal saboteur and rejected self will also gain plenty of evidence that it is not worthwhile to relate in a healthy way.

– "You behave yourself professionally." Professional behaviour not only means "turning up on time" in a consistent and reliable way, but also means speaking thoughtfully and carefully about the most urgent issues for the patient. Simply remembering that the patient is a person whose mind has been devastated by one of the worst illnesses in medicine lets him know that you are there for his needs, not yours. What can be helpful is taking the lead from what the patient says first rather than the traditional interrogative questioning of "How are you?" Pausing for a few moments to listen to what the patient needs can lead to an exploration of the subjective distress that he carries in his distressed state of mind. Self-disclosure is kept to a minimum to avoid the idea that the professional is there to have her needs met, rather than the patient's.

– "You concern yourself with the patient's problems." As stated above, the needs of the patient come first. This is not easy to follow, most of all because we as mental health professionals have a natural need for the patient to change and show improvements to meet our needs to be valued (Kapur, 2014). However, stepping back to "wait and see" and capture the patient's state of mind will give the patient the idea that the primary concern is for his needs, not yours.

– "You accept being in the position of a subjective object in the client's life, while at the same time you keep both your feet on the ground." The turbulence of the internal world of the patient will often mean we could be persuaded to act out all sorts of "manic" behaviour (Lucas, 2009) rather than keeping our feet on the ground and employing reliable, consistent, and thoughtful measures to concentrate on the emotional state of the patient.

– "You accept love and even in the in-love state, without flinching and without acting-out your response." As stated in Chapter One of this book, the helper is at the receiving end of powerful projections and projective identifications, some of which will be overwhelming. Maintaining a steady response in the face of potentially sexualised transference is essential to ensure that the "mad self" of the professional does not collide disastrously with the "mad self" of the patient with the promise of a magic cure for the distress caused by severe mental illness.

– "You accept hate and meet it with strength rather than with revenge." The idea of the "Brick Mother" is often discussed in psychiatric settings and the mental health professional has to have the characteristics of "solidity" to deal with the hate and destructiveness so embedded in the internal world of the patient with severe mental illness. Sohn (1985) captures this with his description of the power and strength of the "narcissistic identificate" who believes in his own omnipotence and strength to dominate and destroy others. Support from the multidisciplinary team and good supervision, as well as access to the real "Brick Mother", in the shape of a hospital bed, is essential to survive these projections and not act them out with revenge and retaliation.

– "You tolerate your client's illogicality, unreliability, suspicion, muddle, fecklessness, meanness, etc. and recognise all these unpleasantnesses as symptoms of distress (in private life these same things would make you keep a distance)." I think the characteristics of the paranoid-schizoid so accurately describe the subjective and intersubjective state of the mentally ill patient. Chaotic thinking, impulsivity, hostility, and paranoia prevail and the worker is under immense pressure to maintain any depressive position functioning. As Winnicott so succinctly describes, all of this fragmentation is a consequence of the patient's distress. The internal chaos is reflected in the patient's external world and inevitably projected onto the worker. Here, it is important for the worker to be a "thinking and feeling" container, being able to receive the projections and projective identifications of the patient, while at the same time thinking about the meaning of these emotional events and trying to put into words "who's doing what to whom". Unfortunately, most of these experiences will be negative and thus much work is required to maintain a "contained hope" for the patient's recovery.

– "You are not frightened, nor do you become overcome with guilt feelings when your client goes mad, disintegrates, runs out into the street in a nightdress, attempts suicide or perhaps succeeds. If murder threatens you, call the Police to help out not only yourself, but also the client. In all of these emergencies, you recognise the client's call for help, or a cry of despair because of loss of hope or help." In this final piece of professional advice, I think we can apply Sinason's (1993) conceptualisation of the "mad" and "sane" self. When the "mad self" takes over and is out of control, it displays all the characteristics of Bion's (1959) psychotic personality where destructiveness and sadism predominate. When this "psychic violence" erupts and becomes acted out, then not only should some boundaries be called upon (in the shape of the police or hospitalisation) but also the "sane self" of the worker has to hold on to the hope for the patient and remember that the hostile and paranoid behaviour is driven out of despair. The patient simply cannot help being out of control but requires the worker to hold on to his sanity for him until the patient's own "sane self" returns.

## Order and containment

Therapeutic atmospheres require a clear order where the chaotic and fragmented mind of the patient can be contained. The regularity and consistency are crucial factors to let the patient know he is not only being taken seriously, but also that as an individual, what he says matters and is being thought about. This rule applies from the "top down" for staff and patients. Patients with urgent and unbearable impulses on their mind will feel "peripherised" and "pushed out" if a mental health professional says she is "too busy". The "busy-ness" in the mind of each individual patient is so disturbing that he has become mentally ill. An ordered, thoughtful, and non-persecutory atmosphere takes this seriously. So as to describe the "noise in the internal world" of a patient, I will quote a recent poem by the well-known psychiatrist, Julian Leff (2014) called "Voices".

### Voices

The endless shouting fraught and wild
Voicing the pain of the unloved child
Insidious voices whispering, mocking
Blaming and shaming for something shocking
Neighbours' voices through paper-thin walls
Sneering and jeering with harsh cat-calls
Shouts from people passing by
Who know the secrets that make you cry
Accusations from those long-dead

> Accessing thoughts within your head
> In darkest night the threats of violence
> The pills that promise endless silence

I think Leff gives a very graphic account of the intensity of persecutory objects that the patient with severe mental illness lives with. Creating an atmosphere of "non-persecutory, understanding and ordered voices" gives the patient some easing of his distress. Most of all, it minimises the possibility of the external world mirroring the internal world of the patient, which then gives the "sane self" of the patient an idea that he can be helped.

## Envy and narcissism

Both of these characteristics are salient features of paranoid-schizoid functioning and thus reflective of the states of mind of severely mentally ill patients. In commenting on creating the optimum therapeutic atmosphere, I will look at these aspects from the perspective of staff and patients. First, from a staff and helper's point of view there is the ordinary narcissism of healthcare best described by Brenman (2006):

> The analytic setting is arranged as the best means we know of pursuing psychic truth, yet we arrange fees and times for our benefit as well as the patient's. We pursue knowledge, partly for our own interest and we are pleased if our patients do well and develop. We obtain satisfaction from the patient's development and whether worked or not, the patient knows this. Indeed to deny this would be to refute the patient's contribution to our lives ... (p. 2)

And so to the reality of mental health and social care. Staff obtain their livelihoods out of the existence of people with severe mental health illness. Our careers depend on it. So the patient who comes to us knows we are there because of him. While this is no different to other areas of healthcare, the area of severe mental illness has a particular aspect where every part of the patient's life is disabled by the illness. So potentially a very vulnerable and damaged patient is in a position of having to feed the narcissism of a professional's "healthy life". As one psychotic patient said to me, "I can hardly get up in the morning, my mind is ravaged by voices and I'm supposed to make you feel OK by showing you I'm feeling better, when I'm not."

So what of the worker's narcissism in a therapeutic atmosphere?

I think it has to have the following characteristic: "No pressure, no desire!" One of the dictums of the psychoanalyst Wilfred Bion (1957) when working with patients is "No memory, no desire". In other words, enter the world of the patient with no expectation that they have to give *you* something. An internal world characterised by persecution and anxiety will often find the simplest of requests as a violent intrusion on the patient's mind. As Steiner (1993) so aptly describes it is how the patient *experiences* what you say and do that determines the progress of any emotional work. For example, this is a recent account of an incident involving a sixty-five-year-old male patient suffering from chronic schizophrenia in one of Threshold's projects:

> At 10pm the patient appeared in a highly distressed state and asked staff to help him kill himself. He asked staff members to find him a rope as he wished to hang himself. He stated that his life is not worth living and he is going to end it now. He stated voices had tortured him with telling him to kill himself. He stated that he could not fight them anymore. He had been approaching staff begging for help to end his life.

So what do you say and what do you do to best help this patient, with a minimum of pressure and desire?

Via projective identification (from staff to patient, or "introjective identification"), we convey without words a concern for his "sane self" trapped by his "mad self" that convinces him the only way to end the torture of his voices is to kill himself (Rosenfeld, 1987). We then choose our words carefully, all the time focusing on:

- Making the patient feel better, rather than focusing on lessening *our* anxieties in managing this high risk situation.
- Minimising the possibility that our words will be experienced as harsh and persecutory by an internal world that must feel like a "living hell".
- Speaking simply, but compassionately.

Some suggestions are:

- Quietness, for say ten to thirty seconds, followed by, "You have no one or nothing in your mind to stop you feeling like this?"
- "Not only are we here to help you with this 'fight' to stay alive, but we will make sure you're not on your own for the rest of the night".
- "We are here to make sure you stay alive".

The essence of these comments is to let the patient know he is not alone against the ferocity of this internal battle between "life and death" and that we know his "sane self" is trapped by his "mad self". We will be his "sane self" as represented by the staff team, the project, and ultimately the agency, Threshold, headed by myself as the CEO. I purposely "make it my business" to meet with patients once a year and make two to three visits to each of Threshold's six residential projects, to let them know that in the "Threshold atmosphere there is someone looking after their "home" and "looking out for them" if things go wrong. Security and firmness characterise the overall atmosphere essential for patients to feel safe.

Finally, I will turn to the narcissism and envy within the patient's state of mind. The assumption in this theoretical framework is that destructive narcissism is present to some extent in all patients with severe mental illness. I think this can often be seen in their first presentation in a psychiatric setting, where the clinical features are not impaired by sedative medication. I will take an excerpt from the work of Herbert Rosenfeld (1971a) to illustrate processes that I believe come alive outside, as well as inside the consulting room:

> When the psychotic patient living in a state of fusion with the analyst begins to experience himself as a separate person, violent destructive impulses make their appearance. His aggressive impulses are sometimes an expression of anger related to separation anxiety, but generally, they have a distinctly envious character. (p. 123)

Outside the consulting room and in creating a therapeutic atmosphere, I think it is crucial that staff are cognisant of the violent eruptions that can occur when "separateness" occurs, whether that be staff finishing their working day/shift, weekend breaks, or holidays. Unwittingly, psychotic patients will "merge" with staff in their phantasy life. Any separation is felt to be too much and there emerges an acting out of envious impulses from an object damaged, impoverished, and wrecked by his own internal world. Sensitivity to separations is crucial to let the patient know he has been understood and, where appropriate, putting words to the patient's state of mind in relation to staff "comings and goings" can maximise a feeling of being understood and thus lessen the chance of acting out.

# CHAPTER THREE

# Group processes

Whether it is in a mental health hostel, psychiatric ward, day hospital, or social care setting, group processes are always operating and have a profound influence on the day-to-day running of services for people with severe mental illness. This chapter will outline the three predominant theories of group psychotherapy that are used to understand how groups work, both informally and formally, and then go on to analyse clinical situations where these theories can help us understand the complexity of interactions, particularly between staff and patients.

## Bion and groups

At the appointed time, members of the group begin to arrive: individuals engage each other in conversation for a short time, and then, when a certain number has collected, a silence falls on the group. After a while desultory conversation breaks out again, and then another silence falls, it becomes clear to me that I am, in some sense, the focus of attention in the group. Furthermore, I am aware of feeling uneasily that I am expected to do something. At this

point I confide my anxieties to the group, remarking that, however
mistaken my attitude might be, I feel just this. (Bion, 1961, p. 30)

So begins a whole new style, a theoretical and technical approach to
working with groups. By adopting the stance of a psychoanalyst
trained in working intensively (up to five times per week) with individuals, in the group, Bion is creating a regressive atmosphere whereby
the individual states of mind can be observed, particularly as they relate
to him as the group leader. As a master of gathering the transference
(Riesenberg-Malcolm, 1986) he immediately comments on how he
has become the object of interest with such comments, in reply to an
inquisitive group member, as:

> ... for Mr. X who is anxious for the welfare of the group, quite
> rightly turns his attention to the source of the trouble, which, from
> his point of view, is myself. You can see that he has a very good idea
> of tackling at once those elements of his group which are destruc-
> tive of morale and good fellowship. He, therefore, asks me directly
> what my object is and why I can't give a straightforward explana-
> tion of my behaviour. I can only apologise and say that, beyond
> feeling that the statement I want to study group tensions is prob-
> ably a very inadequate description of my motives, I can throw no
> light on the problem. (1961, p. 32)

It was from this group, run at the Tavistock Centre, that Bion conceptu-
alised group mentalities or "states of mind" that can operate at any one
time in a group, small or large. The dysfunctional groups were driven
by pathological "basic assumptions" that are the underlying drive
for group members to relate to each other and the group leader. I will
describe these states of mind and then go on to outline the more functional and effective "work group" mentality.

### Dependency

In this state the group members are wholly dependent on the group
leader for all the answers and solutions to their problems. This "dependency group" sees the leader as omnipotent, while considering other
group members as inadequate, immature, and incompetent. There is
an idealisation of the leader with efforts to steal the leader's goodness.

The failure of the leader to live up to these expectations is matched by denial and then a disappointment which leads to a devaluation and then an urge to find an alternative. Envy and greed are also characteristics of this group's "state of mind" and often group members can feel they have a common enemy in hating the leader, who does not deliver "miracles" and take away their distress.

## Fight—flight group

In this group there is an impulse to either fight with each other or flee from a perceived external threat. Subgroups develop that can either fight with the group leader or each other. There is a hostile and paranoid relationship to the group leader, either in feeling controlled by him or wanting to control him. Projection and projective identification are prevalent with little or no capacity to think through disturbing and difficult emotions.

## Pairing

Often, couples, which may or may not be heterosexual, emerge in a bid to reproduce and provide an entity that can take over and usurp the group leader. This "magical sexual phantasy" is aimed at creating an entity that will take away the distress and disturbance in the group. Sexualised and overexcited pairings are seen as the cure for the group's ills.

As an alternative to this dysfunctional pathological functioning, much of which represents the features of the paranoid-schizoid position (see Chapter One), there exists the possibility of the "work group", which Bion (1961) describes as:

> ... the "sophisticated group" ... called the "work group". The name is short and expresses well an important aspect of the phenomena I wish to describe, so that in future, I shall use the term "sophisticated group". When a group meets, it meets for a specific task and in most human activities today co-operation has to be achieved by sophisticated means ... . The capacity for co-operation on this level is great as anybody's experience of groups will show. But it is so different in mind from the capacity for co-operation which is evident on the basic assumption level. (p. 98)

Essentially, this refers to the "here and now" emotional engagement of the group in pursuing its primary task. External reality has to be managed in the spirit of talking and thinking through the different tasks in any group. The particular task of the leader is to be aware of the destructiveness of basic assumption functioning and make comments which maximise the possibility of full emotional contact between all the group members.

## Yalom and groups

Irving Yalom, one of the pioneers of group psychotherapy (Yalom, 1970) adopts a very different style and theoretical framework to that of Wilfred Bion. The main strength of Yalom's approach is his conceptualisation of eleven therapeutic factors which he proposes are essential for effective group psychotherapy. I originally studied these with colleagues in the late 1980s (Kapur, Miller, & Mitchell, 1988), when I adopted this model in working with inpatient and outpatient populations. I will describe these factors in more detail, referring to Yalom's most recent text (Yalom & Leszcz, 2005) and then use clinical material to illustrate how they can be helpful in working with large and small groups of people with severe mental illness.

1. **Installation of Hope**
   The installation of hope (not unlike the rationale adopted in the traditional "recovery" model) is seen as crucial in conducting groups and giving the patient a clear idea that change is possible. In this particular model any signs of hope, in either the individual or group, are used to maintain a positive atmosphere.

2. **Universality**
   This feeling of "being in the same boat" is one of the most powerful therapeutic factors to ease the feeling of isolation that accompanies moderate or severe mental illness. Often this experience can allow group members to express their feelings more easily as they no longer feel they are the only ones that have particular symptoms or difficulties.

3. **Imparting information**
   Here, Yalom refers to both didactic instruction or more directive interventions and direct advice. The former refers to the psycho-educational nature of groups, such as Alcoholics Anonymous, where

particular information is given on the negative effects of alcohol misuse. Potentially, this lessens the anxiety of group members as it lessens uncertainty about particular diagnoses. Direct advice refers to particular suggestions that the group leader may put forward to overcome a particular problem. It may also be that the process of giving advice, rather than the context of it, is beneficial by implying and conveying mutual interest and caring.

4. **Altruism**

The interpersonal act of helping others, out of a sense of generosity and wish to be helpful, is seen as an important therapeutic factor. Inter-group member altruistic acts not only benefit the receiver, but are also felt to be beneficial to those offering help as they may feel they are of worth to others.

5. **The Corrective recapitulation of the primary family group**

The existence of any group, formal or informal, small or large, will inevitably lead to a re-enactment of memories and experiences of the original family group. Sibling rivalries may develop between group members and there will also be an arousal of parental experiences towards the group leader(s). The idea behind this factor is that there is a correction of early family conflicts which can take place by working through unfinished business from the past. Resolution may lead to more healthy/effective relationships.

6. **Development of socialising techniques**

The development of basic social skills is seen as a key ingredient of effective group therapy. Often group members will learn how to be responsive to others, manage conflict resolution more effectively, be less likely to be judgemental of others, and they can become more capable of experiencing and expressing accurate empathy.

7. **Imitative behaviour**

An identification with the behaviour of the group leader or other group members may help individuals explore new and more helpful ways of relating to others. This may be helpful around issues such as self-disclosure where group members can feel more at ease sharing thoughts and feelings when they see others doing the same.

8. **Interpersonal learning**

In this particular model of group therapy, interpersonal relatedness is seen as an important element of group members exploring their impact on others and their view of themselves. In particular, if group members have "disturbed views of themselves", these can potentially be corrected through interpersonal feedback. Here the task of the group leader is to explicitly facilitate feedback between group members so they can "see how others see them" and potentially correct any maladaptive behaviours. In describing this factor, Yalom & Leszcz (2005) rely on the work of Harry Stack Sullivan and his interpersonal theory of psychiatry (1962) which stresses the importance of interpersonal attachments as a way of improving the patient's "sense of life".

With this factor there is also the role of the "corrective emotional experience" (Alexander & French, 1946) which is proposed to repair the trauma of past relationships. Yalom and Leszcz (2005, p. 29) list the main components of this corrective emotional experience in ...

- A group supportive enough to permit this risk taking.
- Reality testing, which allows the individual to examine the incident with the aid of consensual validation from other group members.
- Recognition of the inappropriateness of certain interpersonal feelings and behaviour or of the inappropriateness of avoiding certain interpersonal behaviour.
- Ultimate facilitation ... of the individual's ability to interact with others more deeply and honestly.

For Yalom, group psychotherapy is effective where there is a strong interpersonal engagement in the group and the emergence of learning about oneself from this group process. As individual interpersonal styles emerge in the group, there can be modifications in this social microcosm, so giving individuals an opportunity to explore newer and perhaps more effective interpersonal behaviours.

Finally, for this particular factor, Yalom comments on the importance of transference distortion being corrected through thought. By this he means that if group members, particularly the leader, are named in a distorted way linked to past traumatic experiences, then some understanding of this incorrect view may help the group member see the other person "as he really is", rather than someone from the past. Thus, distortions are corrected and the group member can manage his relationships without the prejudice of the past.

9. **Group cohesiveness**

This is one of the most important therapeutic factors in groups. It is defined as a sense of belonging in a group. Such a group retains good inter-member attractiveness and acceptance with members feeling the comfort and warmth of the group. There is one caveat against this factor; an over-cohesive group can become like a "closed cult" with little heterogeneity among group members, so lessening the exploration of healthy inter-member differences that can lead to new ideas and experiences.

10. **Catharsis**

This factor is linked to other therapeutic factors and refers to group members being able to "get things off their chest" and express positive and negative feelings to group members and the leaders. This can be the fuel for interpersonal learning and other processes which bring the group alive and make it a "learning and corrective" group experience.

11. **Existential factors**

This final factor refers to the issues in everyday life, such as the acceptance of solitude, the inevitable "highs and lows" in life, taking responsibility for one's actions, and recognising that at times life can be unfair and unjust. This factor is seen to interweave with the other processes described above.

## Foulkes and groups

A theoretical exposition of the work of S. H. Foulkes is difficult as Foulkes does not clearly demarcate any specific theoretical constructs (as Yalom and Bion do), but rather seems to base his model (1964) on the interactive effect of "healthy" group members which can generate group processes that are helpful. Haigh (2013) describes this approach, particularly in respect of therapeutic communities as:

> When this sort of openness is working well, it is difficult to feel paranoid; persecutory fantasies are immediately and deliberately reality-tested. If somebody—staff or community member—feels any anxiety about somebody or not knowing something, then there is a shared acceptance that it is reasonable to challenge others, and

try to understand it through open communication and making contact. This openness is unusual in most adult situations; it refers to the exposure of interpersonal material which is usually left unspoken, maybe communicated non-verbally without full explanation, but normally well beyond where it is possible to allow detailed conversation or scrutiny. Amongst other things, it includes the questioning of motives, the relentless challenging of defences and, inquisitiveness about observable relationships. The defining characteristic is the expectation and demand that communication is more open, more profound and more honest than happens in everyday situations. Through it, relational connections are deepened and personal meaning is found through contact with others. (p. 14)

There is a clear idea in this model that openness will lead to a deeper and more fruitful contact with group members. The emphasis is on the interpersonal engagement with some emotional commitment and self disclosure. While the Foulkesian style does refer to transference to the group leader (Foulkes, 1964), the overall model of what is termed "group analysis" is through this deeper interpersonal engagement of the members of the group. He writes in his 1964 text:

The group recaptures what Erich Fromm calls the "forgotten language". Thus, the area of what the group can share, have in common, communicate, is enlarged in the on-going process of group psychotherapy. Principally, everything happening is considered in its communicational aspect. (p. 69)

In this model, interpretations are mainly group based with the aim of elucidating the underlying meaning of the group state of mind. The communication between the group members, or group matrix, is the raison d'etre of this approach. While not clearly stating the theoretical underpinnings of this approach, with this Freudian approach we can reasonably assume that the emphasis is on the developmental progression of the group to more mature ways of relating, through the interpretative work of the group conductor/leader. I will conclude the review of this particular model with a quote from Foulkes (1964) in the application of these principles in a "mental hospital in peace time":

The attitude of the therapist is decisive, his function catalytic, clarifying, interpretative, especially in regard to defences and resistances. The therapist must understand and accept transference in his own person as well as the whole situation. He should maintain an optimal degree of tension, acting like a thermostat in relation to the emotional temperature of the therapeutic situation. The group configuration is important for the therapist's orientation, but in his interventions and interpretations he must not forget that it is the individual who counts. Improved communication is a good general aim. (p. 215)

I will now analyse two community meetings using the above models of groups. My own expertise, training and experience would be with the work of Bion and Yalom, so my comments on the Foulksian model will be more tentative and gained from a more limited exposure to this particular way of working.

## Containment or empathy

This particular group refers to elderly people with severe mental illness that have been resident in a Threshold therapeutic community. This is a weekly meeting which lasts for one hour and has five staff and seven patients (twelve in total). I will report on segments of a process recording followed by my own analysis. Six of the seven patients suffer from a psychotic disorder, with one patient also having a diagnosis of learning disability and psychotic disorder. This group opens with:

PT. 1:      "What was that woman's name that was here yesterday?"
STAFF 1:   Replies with name.
PT. 1:      "Is she coming to live here. Where is she?"
STAFF 1:   "She is in the psychiatric hospital, and that was her first visit, she comes from New Zealand."
PT. 2:      "My aunt who lives in New Zealand died of cancer a few months ago, my mum is the only one left now."

### Analysis

In these five interchanges we can pick out the following themes:

– There is an interest from the patient in a new arrival to the community. Could this represent some insecurity about the arrival of a new group member as to whether they would settle the community?

- The staff member replies normally, with an interactive response, although a comment could have been offered exploring the patient and the group's anxiety of someone new joining the group.
- The patient enquires as to where she is and where her future might be.
- The staff member replies, again in an interactive way, giving details of her origins; where she is now and the nature of her visit. An alternative could have been to offer a comment around how her proposed existence or life in the community may bring its own fears and hopes.
- Another patient replies by "associating" to a relative that had lived in the same country, subsequently dying of cancer with the disclosure that her mum is still alive.

At this early stage of the group, several things may be occurring. Interactively and interpersonally there is an interest in a possible new group member who may or may not become a member of the family (Yalom's therapeutic factor of re-enactment of earlier family roles as well as a sense of cohesiveness, belonging, or a wish to belong) emerging in the group. For a Foulkesian perspective there is evidence of good early communication in the group. While so far staff members have responded interactively, usually with answers, an alternative interpretative response could be:

> "I think there are some worries in the group/community about who might join us? You might be worried about whether this person will do well with us, or whether they may not be with us or stay with us for too long."

What I am trying to capture here are the underlying anxieties about what the group may do with new members—accept them or kill them off. By putting words to what may be powerful primitive anxieties, the group may then be able to deepen its understanding of members' own fears of what they may do for themselves and others. The next segment is:

The group continues ...

STAFF 1:   "She still has you."
  PT. 2:   "Do you mean her own sisters and brothers?"
STAFF 2:   "K will be starting on Monday, she is our new staff member, do people remember her? Lots of new faces around."

PT. 3:    "Yeah, lots of new faces."

STAFF 2:    "Patient A is not a new face to you (speaking to Patient C), but others may not know her."

STAFF 1:    "Lots of connections with the residents here from other houses. There has been a lot of loss here for people and loss for you too (addressing Patient 1)."

PT. 2:    "Yes, mum is on her own. You know my mum did something when I was thirteen, she got us to write to dad saying we did not want to see him again, as he had walked out and she wanted a divorce. I was too young to know what I was doing".

STAFF 2:    "Do you regret that?"

## Analysis

- The initial interaction, while relating to the original family scene, may have a reference to whatever happens in the group/community; there will still be group members (sisters and brothers) available to be with or help this patient.
- The second staff member then introduces the idea of a new staff arrival, with potential new siblings/parents.
- Staff member 1 then goes on to address existing connections to other projects and residents of this project and noting also the losses that have taken place.
- Patient 1 then speaks about regrets of rejecting her father, on her mother's instruction before a divorce.

As the group progresses, we see Yalom's factor of "family re-enactment" becoming apparent with sisters, parents, and others being spoken about. There is the theme of new arrivals and the breaking up of relationships. We can also see the presence of the "universality" factor with patients empathising over loss (the experience of "being in the same boat"). The Foulkesian idea of active interaction and inter-member engagement continues. Loss is very much in the atmosphere and what occurs when relationships break down. A comment to capture this could be:

> "Lots of comings and goings in the community. Perhaps also a worry as to how staff can hold the community together and can look after people if things break down."

Here I am, trying to capture the anxieties about the group/community being a "container" for comings, goings, and breakdowns. Will the staff be sensitive and strong enough to make sure that those who leave/divorce can be thought about in a helpful way, rather than forgotten about?

And in the next phase of the group:

PT. 2:     "Yes, I do regret it, it wasn't fair, she made us do that. My dad worked for the D.O.E. (Department of the Environment). I missed him. My mum treats my kids like shit and my husband turned my kids against me."

STAFF 3:  "You feel used?"

PT. 2:     Yes, he used me and still tries to, but I stand up to him. Did you know I lost two wee boys, both on Good Friday with a year between them? I lost two other boys as well. I have three daughters."

## Analysis

– Patient 2 continues to describe the loss of the relationship with her father and the emotional abuse of her kids.
– Staff agree and try to empathise.
– The patient continues to complain about being "used and abused" by those close to her.
– This excerpt finishes with the patient reporting the loss of her two sons (I assume to illness) and with her still having three daughters.

Keeping in mind Yalom's therapeutic factors, we can see that "existential factors" are being explored, particularly in respect of unhappy relationships and loss. There emerges a theme of loss, both in terms of family well-being/goodness and death. Perhaps there is also a possibility that the patients/community may also be worried about whose needs are being met in this setting and could there be a possibility that this patient is communicating something about the potentially abusive atmosphere in the community? A group as a whole interpretation could be:

> "You have talked about kids not being treated well, feelings of being 'used and abused' for the needs of others. Maybe people in the group get a bit worried that as staff, we might do that to

you—not looking after 'parts of you' well, getting paid to do a job
to look after you, but maybe you're not feeling 'looked after' ."

While not specifically referring to any of Bion's basic assumptions,
I think what may be occurring in the "state of mind" of the group is
a primitive anxiety that the vulnerable parts of patients would not be
looked after by staff. This could trigger the "flight/fight" basic assumption where there is a strong underlying fear of those in authority not
protecting patients from destructive elements in the group.
    The group continues ...

STAFF 3:   "That must have been heartbreaking for you?"
   PT. 2:   "I had good neighbours."
STAFF 1:   "Loss can bring up a lot for people."
   PT. 2:   "The hospital said the boys were too heavy."
STAFF 2:   "It was hard to lose all your boys."

## Analysis

– Patients and staff continue to explore this existential issue, with a
  theme of loss appearing as a strong feature in this group.
– There emerges an idea from the patient that the "boys were too heavy
  for the hospital", suggesting they were overweight and died as a
  result.

The issue and meaning of loss is clearly a major theme in the group and
this is picked up and understood by the staff present. However, as with
my other suggestions, it could be that the primitive anxieties are very
much present and could be captured by the following comment:

> "Clearly there are lots of feelings to do with people losing others in
> relationships and in life. Maybe there are lots of strong feelings in
> the group about this and you are not sure whether they might be
> 'too heavy' for staff to manage. You want to speak about them but
> are worried we can't handle them?"

Again, what I am suggesting is that in the "container/contained" relationship there is a primitive anxiety that powerful feelings cannot be
spoken about. Patients may feel that their "madness is too much for the

staff" to manage. Elucidating these anxieties could help patients say what they really think and feel.

The group continues ...

STAFF 1:   "I am aware of the loss you all had last November, with W and J passing away."

STAFF 2:   "Yes, it was difficult."

STAFF 4:   "There have been a lot of changes over the past few years; the house had been very settled for a long time, then people started to move: lots of changes in the whole community."

PT. 1:   "Lots of changes, how is R.B.?"

STAFF 4:   "He is OK, I'm sure it was strange after R.B. and J.M. and C.M. all going within six months of each other?"

## Analysis

– The theme of loss continues, mainly taken up by staff in a sympathetic way, so maximising the therapeutic factors of cohesiveness, universality, and existential issues.

– The patient enquires as to the welfare of R.B.

Interpersonal engagement continues well in this group with the "state of mind" of the group continuing to focus on loss. However, as stated above, there could be more attention paid to the idea of how the community, particularly staff, are containing the anxieties of the patient group. For example, a comment could be made such as:

> "I guess staff act as 'caretakers' for you all. Maybe you feel we look after people well until 'life takes them', though you might get a bit worried that we don't look after them properly and they become unwell."

Addressing these deeper anxieties could help explore the phantasies/ realities of how patients feel they are being looked after, or otherwise.

In summary, we can see that all the theoretical ideas expressed by Yalom, Foulkes, and Bion are illustrated in this community/group meeting. What I am particularly highlighting is that by addressing deeper anxieties about containment, the more disturbing feelings about how severely mentally ill patients are being cared for can be verbalised, so creating a "therapeutic atmosphere" that takes seriously the underlying fear of patients with severe mental illness.

## Can anyone see what is going on?

This group refers to a community meeting in a supported housing setting that looks after people with severe mental illness. There are six staff and eleven patients in this group. All patients have a diagnosis of psychosis and are usually resident for between two and three years. Ages range fromthirty to fifty-five, with seven males and four females.

STAFF 1:   Patient A is still in psychiatric hospital. Staff have been up to see her and the manager and I are going up tomorrow. I'm just wondering how people are feeling about this?"

PT. 1:   "Wouldn't like to be in hospital, very scary."

PT. 2:   "She's very young, is there any sign of her getting out?"

PT. 3:   "I've been visiting in those places before. They do their best, but it's a place that gets you down".

PT. 4:   "I look at it differently. It's a place to get you better. They are keen for you to get out, it's not a case of them holding you back—they want you to get better."

PT. 3:   "I don't mean ill will, there is a sad air about the place."

PT. 4:   "I know you don't, I have fond memories there."

PT. 3:   "You are in deep thought (directed to staff member 1)."

STAFF 1:   "I am".

**Silence, one minute.**

PT. 1:   "I don't like psychiatric hospital, I used to like another hospital, but didn't the last two times in it. As Patient 4 said, it's a place to rest, but last two times I didn't like it."

**Silence, one minute.**

PT. 3:   "Who is going tomorrow?"

STAFF 1:   "The manager and I."

PT. 5:   "Will I get her a card?"

PT. 6:   "I did get her a card but don't know where it is."

STAFF 1:   "I think another patient got a card and … It feels like there is a fear we can't keep people safe here."

## Analysis

- The group starts with an interest in a patient who has been hospitalised.
- Patients have mixed feelings about how good or bad psychiatric hospitals may be.
- There is a wish to make contact with the patient through a staff visit and card.

I think staff member 1 does capture the anxieties in the group by exploring whether people can be kept safe at the project or break down. There is an anxiety around illness and how people will be looked after (existential issues and universality). The prevailing atmosphere is characterised by what happens when people break down and can a good or a bad psychiatric setting put them "back together" again. Also, will the therapeutic community in which they live be able to do this and prevent further relapse? A comment to this effect may be:

> "I think you have mixed feelings about how good or bad hospitals may be, but most of all you are worried how we might prevent any breakdown, or if a breakdown occurs will we be able to put you back together again."

I think this is where Bion's model and the theoretical approach detailed in Chapter One are most helpful. This comment by the staff member/group leader would attend to the subjective experiences of disintegration so succinctly covered in this theoretical framework in working with people with severe mental illness (Jackson, 2001). If people with psychosis believe that efforts are being made to address this inner reality, they feel the atmosphere is indeed therapeutic.

**The group continues …**

PT. 5:   "We aren't to blame: if somebody is going to take unwell, they will."

STAFF 1:   "I meant staff."

PT. 4:   "I had an email from a friend. It sounds like it's off track but it's of relevance . He is very anxious and his thing is that he should be able to cope. It is very difficult reaching out when unwell. I told him that he needs to seek professional help. In my experience, I say to myself it's only a phase but you may need to be in hospital. You see it with physical illness but with mental illness it's an underlying embarrassment, stigma."

PT. 3:    "Did he talk to friends and family about this?"

PT. 4:    "No, because I think he knows what I have been through. I advised him to go and see a professional. He's concerned the GP might laugh."

PT. 3:    "Highly unlikely a GP would laugh and wouldn't reflect well on them."

PT. 2:    "It's not a comment on a person's suffering but a GP's attitude."

PT. 4:    "Exactly, laughing inappropriately, and I wonder what they have done to others."

STAFF 1:    "People just end up with labels."

## Analysis

– The discussion moves to seeking help and the positive and negative response from other healthcare professionals.
– The experience of stigma is discussed and how patients can be labelled.

Here, I think we can see how Yalom's factors of universality and cohesiveness are present with patients able to share with each other their common experiences of mental illness. They have a feeling of belonging that lessens feelings of isolation that is so common with people with mental illness. However, what was not addressed was how the staff may be seen in the same way as other professionals.

An alternative comment could be:

> "I think you get worried as to how members of staff would accept or reject you with this label of mental illness. Maybe you are unsure as to whether we could accept and understand you as individual people with this stigmatising diagnosis."

Containment does require detailed attention to how patients think and feel about staff, so they can begin to explore in a serious way the anxieties about how staff will treat them. After all, patients are placing their vulnerabilities in the hands/minds of staff, who are entrusted to look after them. Attention to this would not only ensure a "work group" but also lessen the possibility of staff rejecting the feelings of patients, either by dismissing (collapsing) or criticising (persecuting) patients for their disturbed state of mind.

The group continues ...

PT. 8:     "It says it happens to 25% of people. We know we aren't well. There are people out there who think they are normal, but they aren't."

STAFF 1:   "Being insightful helps, others can't recognise it."

PT. 8:     "Self-diagnosis, self-medicating, very vicious spiral to get into. Not suggesting all professionals are perfect but they have nothing to gain from prescribing/not prescribing. Experts in our general condition. We are experts on our own. Together it is a very good combination or can be."

**Silence, one minute**

PT. 1:     "It worries me because I could take it at any minute. Well at the minute, but could relapse."

PT. 4:     "There were no signs E. was unwell."

PT. 1:     "I think I saw a few, but don't want to say here".

STAFF 1:   "I hear you saying that you could be ill but nobody would know. Maybe other people are saying what they see?"

PT. 4:     "People knew her better than me."

STAFF 1:   "I think there is a fear that any of us could be unwell and not know: what happens when we are left on our own."

PT. 1:     "I don't like to admit when I'm not well."

STAFF 2:   "You're scared if you talk, you would end up in hospital, but there could be another way to handle things."

PT. 6:     "It's worse to bottle it up."

PT. 5:     "I need to talk, if I don't talk about it I end up on the drink and doing something stupid. It's very important to talk, even to someone in the room that you trust. Something to put your faith in."

PT. 7:     "I think this place keeps you out of hospital."

## Analysis

In this interchange:

– There is a recognition that everyone is vulnerable to a mental illness.
– A query as to who is the expert when people break down.

– A worry over re-hospitalisation.
– The importance about talking about "worries" that can lead to mental illness.

While I think there is some evidence of Yalom's factor of universality (everyone is vulnerable to mental illness) along with the existential factor of what it means to have a mental illness, I think the essence of this final interchange in the group is about the quality of containment that may or may not be provided. A different staff intervention to deal with this issue could be:

> "I think you feel vulnerable with this condition, mental illness, but
> I think your biggest vulnerability/fear is whether we are able to
> listen to, and take seriously, the thoughts and feelings that drive
> you "mad". Can we as a staff group handle it?"

The theoretical framework detailed in Chapter One clearly points to containment of paranoid anxieties and hostile feelings as the key element of therapeutic effectiveness. This is not to take away from the value of the Yalom and Foulkes models of group psychotherapy. Rather, in working with groups of severely mentally ill patients, I think the predominant therapeutic need in the projective/introjective cycle is how the patient, suffering from the subjective experiences of a mentally ill state of mind, can have an experience of his most distressing feelings recognised and verbalised in that "therapeutic moment". I think if this occurs (as my research cites in Chapter Six) there is a chance that this most terrifying of human experiences will be eased and the patient will improve, subjectively and symptomatically.

# CHAPTER FOUR

# Individual processes

I will present several cases in this chapter that adopt the theoretical basis outlined in the Introduction and Chapter One. I will use clinical material to illustrate how, once captured, a simple but detailed analysis of the patient's state of mind can be of enormous help for the mental health professional in working out what is the best way to relate to the patient, in formal and informal settings.

## Case 1: psychosis, abuse and loss

L is a fifty-four-year-old female patient who has suffered from schizophrenia for most of her adult life. She resides in one of Threshold's "supported living" projects, which has a staff team of six, and sixteen patients. The interchange to be presented is from a young, newly recruited member of staff, who has seen this patient in "key-work" for twelve consecutive sessions. The patient has been in psychiatric hospital on many occasions. This new keyworker has taken over from another member of staff who had left abruptly and had delivered only two key-work sessions.

This is usually all the background information I require before hearing the interchanges. Several other staff members are present in this case discussion.

The patient arrives ten minutes late, having been previously dressed in a "flimsy" or a "onesy" which is a pyjama type garment (this was noticed by the keyworker before the session started). The patient is now more appropriately dressed.

> PT.:    "Hi, sorry I'm late. I had to change my clothes out of that 'flimsy'. It was all a bit of a rush .... Anyway, do you know if that little boy who lives nearby who died of cancer has been buried yet?"
>
> KEYWORKER:    "Yes, I think so."

## Analysis

In this keyworker arrangement, we have a severely mentally ill and damaged patient in the middle to late stages of her life in the room with a young enthusiastic member of staff. We have a situation where a damaged state of mind is being placed "face to face" with someone employed to look after her in a helping role.

The staff group discuss this further. This is a patient who emotionally suffers all the turmoil of the paranoid-schizoid position with her mind characterised by damaged objects that have "driven her mad". Repeated hospitalisations over thirty years characterise a state of mind that frequently breaks down. Potentially (as listed in Table 1) there could be a destructive envious and spoiling attack on the keyworker. The arrangement with two people at opposite ends of the mental health spectrum, as well as their timeline of life, means that powerful projections and projective identifications may be triggered towards the keyworker. With her psychiatric history (and as we shall see later, her personal history) there are many experiences of abandonment and loss. Potentially, she will carry around with her profound feelings of emptiness and a feeling of being totally disconnected from others.

So, immediately, the damaged state of mind may be violently activated, leaving the keyworker vulnerable to negative processes. The keyworker (in the countertransference) reported being in the room with someone who was keen to attend but perhaps (as indicated by her ten minute lateness) is holding a lot back for fear of damaging this new member of staff. Other staff in the group corroborate this analysis. A state of mind wanting to co-operate but holding a lot back.

From the initial interchange we could also infer:

- Originally dressed in a "flimsy/onesy" could be associated with flimsy/chaotic/barely held-together behaviour, which may capture her state of mind.
- Her attempt to dress more appropriately may indicate her own efforts to bring order to her state of mind. To "tidy things up" herself for her new keyworker.
- The links to the little boy who died of cancer may indicate her close identification with loss and an idea that she knows what it feels like to lose people in her life.

An alternative comment is suggested by myself and the group:

> "I think you are making an effort to make things better, work with me, work with other staff but perhaps you feel you have to bring all these things together by yourself?"

While no reference is made to the death of the young boy with cancer (technically, I think it is too much to add another theme when speaking to this disturbed state of mind), the staff do become aware of the depth and breadth of loss this patient has experienced. In her life she has suffered:

- Loss of her own natural parents as she was adopted at an early age.
- Sexual abuse by her uncle (which is currently being re-investigated by social services and the police).
- Loss of a daughter and sister to adoption when they were young as she was deemed "as not being able to cope".
- Death of her son to suicide—he suffered from drug addiction.
- Breakdown of her marriage and several relationships.
- Loss of her "sanity".

So, what is the way forward to create a therapeutic atmosphere, formally and informally, to help this patient?

As well as putting words to her state of mind, as illustrated above, I think it is crucial that the atmosphere is characterised by understanding and boundaries. If staff take seriously that the psychic aetiology for her psychosis lies in the history of the emotional, sexual, and physical abuse (which psychiatric literature confirms, e.g., Varese et al., 2012), then staff having a state of mind whereby they understand the impact of these issues can help the patient feel she is being contained. This quality of thinking or alpha-processing could let the patient know via words or introjective identification that,

- Carrying such huge multiple losses in her mind has driven her mad.
- Maybe she has never had a chance to mourn the loss of any of these events, a characteristic of the depressive position. Perhaps if she could mourn and work through the loss of one element of these multiple traumas, then she could find some ease.
- The staff and the agency take seriously the impact of these events on her as a person. This humanisation of her could allow her to feel more of a person who has suffered horrific loss.

In further exploration of these issues, staff would also comment on how she can be the "life and soul" of the house, often being overenthusiastic about group trips, new activities in the house, and other events. While this is helpful, I think it is important for staff not to collude with over-excitement as a defence against taking seriously the damage, distress, and despair she carries with her in her internal world. This collusion with her "manic defences" could only further postpone any mourning of what she has lost and offer quick solutions/alleviation of deeply held feelings of love and hate. For this depressive position functioning to occur, staff would have to show considerable concern and understanding of the "mad self trapped by the sane self" (Rosenfeld, 1987; Sinason, 1993) which will act out distress through manic behaviour and destructive attacks on others. Inevitably an over-excited self (Fairbairn, 1952) will attempt to soothe the damaged ego and staff will be unwitting psychic recruits in this. So my further guidance to staff would be:

- Be careful not to get into "happy therapy" to alleviate your anxiety/difficulty in helping the patient.
- Present the patient with a "serious, firm, and thoughtful" state of mind that minimises the chance of collusion with a manic solution to deep-rooted and complex emotional problems.

Overall, I believe that if the atmosphere is characterised by these guidelines, then the patient may slowly link with staff and have an opportunity to work through some elements of the huge loss in her life that has devastated her mind.

## Case 2: keeping you happy from my "fall from grace" into depression

This is a forty-nine-year-old male patient who suffers from psychotic depression. While his last hospitalisation was over twenty years ago, when he was treated with E.C.T. and psychotropic medication (he was hospitalised four times), he has been kept out of hospital with a combination of family support and medication. He had a career in the helping professions which "fell to pieces" in his mid-late twenties, with the onset of his illness. His keyworker has seen him for two months, although with staff rotas can't offer this patient a fixed time every week, so the sessions are somewhat chaotic. Staff report him as a "people pleaser" who is always keen to be compliant and helpful around the residential unit. The death of his mother precipitated his admission to our community care facility. He has a brother and sister and reports his father to be a harsh disciplinarian, who was a sergeant in the army.

The patient arrives on time.

PT.:　"Anything you want to ask me?"
KEYWORKER:　"How have things been for you?"

## Analysis

While the words from the patient seem unremarkable, they do contain important meaning in respect of "who is doing what to whom". In particular, the patient is asking the member of staff what his needs are. Immediately the "tables are turned" and the onus is on the keyworker to disclose what he needs from our patient, rather than vice versa. The observations from staff do suggest that this patient strives to keep others happy, meeting the needs of others, so achieving some kind of pseudo-equilibrium with the world around him. An alternative comment could be:

"I think you're more interested in what I need rather than what you need or want."

I think in this patient's life, he has always put his needs after others'; while this may have "kept the peace" and assuaged any negative reactions of others, it has "pushed him into himself" with little or no opportunity to explore his needs or feelings. Perhaps if the patient could be offered an opportunity, with the above comment, then perhaps he would have a chance to express and explore the depth of feelings associated with the loss of his sanity, career, and ordinary life to severe mental illness. It may be that the "compression" of thoughts and feelings from as long as he can remember has led to a state of mind that is "mad and depressed" (psychotic depression). An experience of a harsh father could only but reinforce an idea that "saying what you really feel and think" would be met by retaliation and persecution. A thoughtful response by the keyworker may open up an opportunity for the patient to "speak about the unspeakable".

The patient replies to the keyworker:

> PT.:      OK, I'm well settled here. I went to see my psychiatrist, but it was a new one and he hadn't read my notes. ... I feel a lot healthier here, I don't eat as much junk food. I did have a lot of health scares but now I feel OK. My mental health has settled after hearing all those voices. The antidepressants seem to be helping me as well."
>
> KEYWORKER:      You get worried about your health and whether you will be OK or not."

## Analysis

I think here the patient is reporting that he has felt at home in the project and feels it is "healthier" for him. As such, he seems to feel a secure base has been provided. However, the psychiatrist has let him down by not reading his notes properly. Perhaps the patient was referring to what may be perceived as the keyworker's "sloppiness" in not offering a fixed time for keywork sessions. The patient may feel "messed about" in this new place which is better for him, where he feels symptomatically and emotionally much better.

I think here, referring to the idea of "container" and "contained", both the keyworker and the patient have a dilemma. Should we keep the perceived "happy state of affairs" or should we say something that tells the patient we know that he may be unhappy with some sloppiness between the two of them, and risk "rocking the boat". The theoretical framework of this approach focuses on the internal world of the patient, which is replete with beta elements, unprocessed emotional particles that when compressed cause the patient so much internal turmoil that he breaks down. Yet, if we don't give him a chance to "decompress" could we not also then be colluding with his psychic disturbance? So I would suggest the alternative words:

> "I think when the psychiatrist hasn't read your notes, you feel not looked after. You might also feel that with me, with the irregular sessions, and may be worried that I will not look after you properly."

Here, I am trying to capture the effects of not being looked after by professionals and those in his personal life.

This patient's "fall from grace" occurred in his late twenties when his life dramatically changed from helper to being helped. The dependency issues became reversed and he is now at the mercy of those looking after him. I think this very real vulnerability is rarely addressed in healthcare, particularly when looking after people with severe mental illness. This patient seems to have coped with this reversal of roles by pleasing others as a way of protecting this vulnerability. However, I think this puts tremendous pressure on the patient's already compressed internal world or container. Perhaps some keywords to understand him could offer some easement and so lessen the enormous pressures on his internal world of "madness and badness".

## Case 3: a wild man finds some roots

One of the key assertions in this text is that *atmosphere is everything*. For many severely mentally ill patients words and human contact are simply too much. Often good work can be done with patients who "live and breathe" the paranoid-schizoid position knowing, intuitively and unconsciously, that they are being looked after in the best possible way. I think the following case illustrates this.

This is a fifty-one-year-old male with a history of hospitalisations with a diagnosis of clinical depression and personality disorder. He has been in the unit for one and a half years, with a six month hospitalisation, when he was actively suicidal. He has a history of chaotic personal relationships with several children from different mothers and pursues hobbies such as horses and looking after animals. He has never held down a regular job. He describes himself as an "evangelical atheist", passionately against any form of religion.

The session begins eight minutes late (the previous session was rearranged by the keyworker, but usually does occur at a fixed point in the week).

>           PT.:   "I didn't get those forms from social security, they said
>                  they sent them but they didn't,"
> KEYWORKER:   "I believe you."

## Analysis

Immediately the patient expresses a disappointment with the system that was there to help him. He speaks as if he wants the keyworker to believe him, which she does. However, already, with the state of mind that is chaotic, he is expressing his dissatisfaction with those around him. Could it be that while Social Security systems have let him down, so have "personal security systems"? Perhaps he has never felt secure in any human relationship and quite understandably has developed a paranoid structure that quickly splits people into very good or very bad. He either idealises or disintegrates people. An alternative comment could have been:

> "The system always seems to let you down. I let you down last
> week with rearranging the session, so maybe you can feel this hap-
> pens everywhere."

This comment may then open up an exploration of his "internal and external systems" of personal and emotional security. The patient continues:

>           PT.:   "I'm reading a good book at the moment. It's about how
>                  all these drugs for schizophrenia don't work and it can
>                  be all put down to a placebo effect. This scientist has
>                  done all of these experiments to prove this. You know
>                  hospitals are just full of fakes. I hate the mental health
>                  system, but I think I have been helped here. You know

I do a lot in the grounds, with the garden and everything.
I like it here.

KEYWORKER:    "You don't trust the mental health system?"

## Analysis

Staff inform me, as well as his keyworker, that this patient exhibits the extreme highs and lows of the paranoid-schizoid position. When he is high he engages in highly charged and overexcited sexual activity and presents as "wild and heroic". However, when he hits a low, he presents as depressed (he has needed ECT) and can then not look after himself. He also splits experiences into good and bad as highlighted by his views on religion. In his time with Threshold he has begun to put down some roots through tending to the garden and being more actively engaged in daily activities. It is as if in his "wild world" characterised by "damaged and dead objects" (Klein, 1952a) which he has managed by overexcited activity (Fairbairn, 1952; Klein, 1952a) he has put some seeds of hope (which have taken root) in the atmosphere provided by staff.

I think small but significant good work has been be completed with this patient by the good links he has made to the project. But will his sane self (Sinason, 1993) feel contented with this, or will his mad self hate the idea of dependency (Rosenfeld, 1987) and find itself attacking and disparaging the "goodness" of the atmosphere. If staff are aware of how this good experience can be toxified or sabotaged (Fairbairn, 1952) because of the internal subjective disturbance of the patient, then they are more likely to held onto the good links that have been established. An alternative comment could be:

> "I think you're never too sure as to whether people are fake or genuine. I think you have made genuine links to us here at Threshold, but I think you are worried that something would spoil this."

To make this comment, it is essential that the atmosphere is as good (as in the depressive position) as is possible. I think we have to convey two things to this patient. First, a genuine concern that we understand the tragic effects of mental illness on him as a person. Second, that we know that mental illness can have such a powerful destructive force on his life. Perhaps an experience of being "held and contained" could lessen this cycle of damage.

### Case 4: rapping my head or rapping your head

If we take seriously the theoretical framework detailed in Chapter One, we can see that severely mentally ill patients live with an intensity of subjective experiences which, at times, are simply unbearable. However, in their personal and professional history, they have had little opportunity to have a safe and reliable container to gain some easement from these "unimaginable storms" (Jackson, 2001). I think the following example illustrates how psychic containers of severely mentally ill patients remain "compressed and toxified" unless they are part of a therapeutic atmosphere that welcomes the thoughts and feelings that cause so much inner turmoil.

This is a thirty-year-old male patient who after previous hospitalisations lived with his mother until he came to Threshold. His journey into the project was characterised by being on the waiting list for a year, the departure of the project manager, a holding arrangement with the deputy project manager where no formal keywork took place, and now facing a new member of staff for the first time since his arrival with us, three months ago. Another twist to this first keywork session is that a cancellation for the member of staff at 3pm meant that he was seen, at his request, an hour earlier than the scheduled 4pm.

After a brief introduction where the member of staff explained that the purpose of the keywork session was to give the patient space to "speak his mind", the keyworker said:

KEYWORKER:    "How are you feeling?"
      PT.:    "Fine."

### Analysis

While the question seems like a reasonable opening, I think it does potentially deprive the patient of an opportunity to speak spontaneously about what may be on his mind. We already know that he has had a "chequered path" into the unit: he was kept waiting for nearly a year and the two parent figures (a project manager and a deputy project manager) let him down. He did not have a smooth entry into the supportive/helping structures in the project. Also, the time of the first keywork session had been changed, which had left the keyworker with a feeling that he "just wanted to get it over and done with".

So alternative comments could have been:

- "You're quiet."
- "Maybe you liked the idea of an earlier time so you could get the keywork session over and done with."

The patient then goes on to say:

> PT.: "All the songs that are in my head, rap songs, people shouting at each other, yelling and cursing. These are voices that are getting worse and I don't really like it. They keep asking me questions about myself and why am I like this when I pass people in the street. I think they are asking me these questions. I think I need to see the psychiatrist to increase my medication to help and cope with the voices."
>
> KEYWORKER: "The rap songs are violent and angry."

## Analysis

I think here the patient is giving us a valuable insight into his state of mind: the "him" that lives with a cruel and sadistic mad self/psychotic personality that violently and cruelly interrogates him and "rips him to pieces". I think he has lived with these voices for as long as he can remember and they have precipitated his initial breakdown in his early twenties. While medication is necessary to help him with this, the "emotional side-effect" has been the lack of opportunity he has had to say what he really thinks and feels, which would be extreme disappointment with Threshold for providing him with an unstable staffing arrangement after one year on a waiting list. It is only when the patient has an opportunity, given by the staff or keyworker, to put into words how he may feel, that the patient can have an idea that a stable and understanding container may be available. It is then and only then that he could achieve some easement by "rapping the mind" of the keyworker so achieving some relief from the torment of his inner world. Alternative comments could be:

"People in your head, shouting, getting worse. Maybe you want to ask questions of me, as to how I could help you, otherwise you feel you need the medication from your psychiatrist to help you with the distress these feelings cause."

Here, I am trying to capture the intensity of distress he contains within himself (beta elements), with the only relief that has been available being the medication. Other human beings in his personal, psychiatric, and Threshold history, have been unavailable/unwilling containers for his madness/rapping. However, if he can be provided with a stable, reliable container, he might be able to put into words the thoughts and feelings that have so disabled him and robbed him of future fulfilment and life and love (see Opalic's (1989) study cited in Chapter Six). This could provide some easement for his troubled and tortured mind.

## Case 5: "Watching you, watching me"

In any human contact between two strangers and indeed, between two people who are together out of their original family setting, there is always an activation of intense thoughts and feelings that belong elsewhere in the recent and past history of the person of being helped. In a mental health setting one stranger is a patient with a container full of disturbing thoughts and feelings (paranoid-schizoid position) in a relationship with a helper, who is trying to do his best to ease the internal pressure caused by these most unpleasant processes.

If we take seriously the above arrangement, then the "space in-between" the helper and the patient will be alive with paranoid and hostile feelings. Most of these will be pushed to the back of the patient's mind (or bottom of the "container") as there will have been little opportunity for a patient with severe mental illness to feel his most disturbing thoughts and feelings have been made welcome. Indeed, while psychotropic medication is of course necessary for the treatment of severe mental illness, a negative side effect, as stated above, is that the patient can feel further pushed back into his mind with nowhere to go with his burdensome emotional life.

I will present a case that illustrates this. This is a fifty-three-year-old male patient who suffers from chronic schizophrenia. He has been in hospital on several occasions as well as being in a previous Threshold project. He has been in this particular project for two years and has settled better in this setting. The keywork history is somewhat fragmented with the member of staff being off sick for two months, and this being the first keywork session after his absence. The keyworker and staff describe him as "huffing" on the return of the former from sick leave. The patient arrives ten minutes late for this first session back.

> PT.:    "Thank you for giving me a hand with the tablets."
> KEYWORKER:    "What do you mean?"

## Analysis

If we take seriously the impact of breaks, particularly sick leave, we can begin to see the huge impact they have on the patient. When a patient's mind is overwhelmed by "damaged objects" it is inevitable that in his phantasy world (Isaacs, 1952) he will believe he has the power to damage others. Indeed, this maybe a magical power which could have been re-enacted on his personal history with parents and others being destroyed or collapsing because of his destructiveness. So keeping this in mind, an alternative comment by the keyworker could be:

> "I think you're glad I've helped you with the tablets, although I guess you must feel I haven't been around to help you with me being on sick leave."

Potentially, this opens up an exploration of the patient's phantasies about how he may feel he has been too much for the keyworker and gives the patient a chance to express his disappointment at the period of absence. So often we can meet our own narcissistic needs of being wanted and valued by the patient (Brenman, 2006) yet we can unwittingly let him down and then of course, the patient withdraws into a well-established psychic retreat (Steiner, 1993).

The session continues:

> PT.:    "My tablets."
> KEYWORKER:    "I think you know I was worried about you. I want to help you to self-medicate as this will help you with more independent living when you leave here. I want you to move on."

## Analysis

In the transference this severely mentally ill patient will have an experience of:

- Being invited into a helping relationship.
- Being let down by the keyworker's two month absence.
- Feeling helped with the right medication to help him manage his difficult and disturbing thoughts and feelings, which may be to do with the keyworker's absence.
- Being encouraged to become more independent and leave the project.

The keyworker also reports that he "wants to work hard to 'shoehorn' the patient into getting better". It may be that this is overcompensating for his absence or he may be acting out the wish for the patient to move on and move as far away as possible from his own disturbed state of mind.

If we take a "helicopter view" we might be able to analyse this situation somewhat differently. Here we have a severely mentally ill patient back in the room with a staff member who has collapsed but feels a great desire to "make things better and help the patient move on". However, the disappointment and phantasies of damage done have not been addressed. So an alternative comment could be:

> "The tablets do help you but maybe they do two other things. They help you deal with unpleasant feelings and thoughts and if you do self-medicate, they push you away from here, particularly me after I've just come back."

The issue of dependency is crucial here. Psychoanalytic clinicians such as Rosenfeld (1987) write of how the patient's hatred of dependency means they enter into a world of self-sufficiency or what Steiner (1993) calls a "psychic retreat". However, the severely mentally ill patient does this for a good reason. The personal and psychiatric history of our patient will be characterised by either collapse or retaliation, not a "contained understanding". If the latter is part of the therapeutic atmosphere the patient may feel more able not only to depend on Threshold, but also form links to a keyworker that may indeed help him on the path to recovery. For this to occur, the nuances of the dependency have to be commented upon, otherwise the patient who has learned to develop a hyper-vigilance to others will inevitably and understandably remain in a world of his own which negates recovery.

## Case 6

PT.:   "It's sunny out there."

## Analysis

Such are the first words of a forty-seven-year-old female patient suffering from paranoid schizophrenia who has just been released from a local psychiatric hospital into our care. In this opening remark to her keyworker (who has just returned from annual leave) we can perhaps formulate some ideas about her state of mind which is anything but sunny.

Whatever the debate about psychiatric nomenclature (as stated in Chapter One) we can gain some insights into the inner world of the patient when a psychiatrist has arrived at such a diagnosis. I think, in psychoanalytic terms, the key feature to be taken from this patient is that she is both "paranoid" and "mad". We can then reasonably assume she will display all the relational features of the paranoid-schizoid position where she will be in a world heavily laden with suspicion and hostility, as well as cut off from others. Other aspects of her personal history are that she has "loved and lost", being a widow (although we do not know the nature of her relationship), and she has a son from her marriage. However, in her late forties, when she should have been enjoying ordinary family life, she has found herself single and diagnosed with a mental illness. Staff also report that she watches them carefully to make sure "she says the right thing and does not upset them". This was my experience on meeting her on one of my regular visits to the project; she waited to tell me how much she "loved it here and staff are wonderful", just two months after being with us. I think it would be reasonable to assume that for any psychiatric patient the initial transition into a community is very difficult for the first six to twelve months, where there is inevitable anxiety of being in a new home. I think we can easily deduce that she is denying the anxieties of living in a community setting with staff who would have been strangers to her. So the keyworker continues.

KEYWORKER:   "Yes it's nice to see it."
        PT.:   "I might go for a walk later, are you on tonight?"

## Analysis

So here we have a keyworker who has just returned from holiday leave (from a livelihood gained from looking after this patient and potentially enjoying a life the patient could have had) having an ordinary discussion about the weather and whether the staff member will be on duty later in the evening.

We can speak to the patient by taking seriously the following aspects of her state of mind:

- The patient has lost out on the joys of adult life through mental illness.
- Watchfulness to please others abounds.
- She is tormented by powerful feelings of paranoia and hostility.
- She has just come from a traditional psychiatric setting where understandably and appropriately, symptoms are treated and lessened, rather than understood.

If we have spoken about these things, I think then I could suggest the following alternative keyworker response:

> "Weather can be good or bad; we can all feel good and bad, and maybe you can feel at times I am here and then not here."

I think this captures how the patient has to keep everything good to deal with the "bad weather" in her mind that she keeps away from staff and the availability or unavailability of staff (the keyworker having just returned from leave).

Keeping primitive feelings "under wraps" is a Herculean task for the patient who is attempting to keep her sanity under enormous internal pressures. A traditional psychiatric setting will give her little opportunity to be contained and so this comment by the keyworker may give the patient an idea that she is not alone with these unbearable feelings.

Another aspect to her story I think also highlights her "loss". This patient leaves the unit on the same day every week to visit her new boyfriend. However, staff have never met him or know anything of his existence. For Valentine's Day she returned to the unit with a ring to say she was engaged and when staff invited her boyfriend to the project she declined the invitation saying she would rather eat out.

I think there is a good chance this is a phantasy boyfriend, but in a very sad way it represents what she has lost to the tragedy of her own life. She has lost both her husband and her sanity and she has to "keep her mind sunny" to avoid letting others see how much paranoia and hostility she lives with. I think this understanding (of her loss) can be integrated into the fabric of the atmosphere we provide for her (formally and informally) to let her see that we understand what she has to contain by herself. Then, and only then, could she put words to her inner turmoil and perhaps get some easement of her tormented state of mind.

## Case 7: "Remember, I can't help it"

The central idea behind Bion's (1957) concept of psychotic and non-psychotic personality or what Rosenfeld (1987) and Sinason (1993) have called the "mad" and "sane" self, is that when one is present, the other is silent. In the case of the "mad self" being present, the "sane self" watches like a spectator as the destructiveness unfolds, helpless to bring an end to this "madness" and hoping it will return to bring some calm and sanity to the patient's life. Alternatively, when the "sane self" is present, the "mad self" can be waiting to pounce and its re-entry into the patient's mind can be triggered by intense feelings of envy, rejection, and exclusion.

In the day-to-day world of psychiatry, I think this conceptual idea can help the staff survive the destructiveness of mental illness and help the patient recover his sane self. This style of understanding the patient's state of mind is captured in Rosenfeld's (1987) description of the "sane dependent self" being captured or tapped by the "mafia gang/mad self" with the patient helplessly watching this hijacking of his sanity. Mental illness, particularly psychotic disorders, are characterised by patients' feeling out of control and "needing to be detained for their own good". If staff can understand the nature of this "takeover" then perhaps the patient can feel more understood and contained. The following piece highlights the conflicts typical of a patient suffering from severe mental illness. This forty-five-year-old male patient has been diagnosed with schizophrenia and has had many hospitalisations.

PT.:    "I've had a really, really rough week, tortured by voices. I had to increase my medication and had to be sedated. I've been up all night. I feel I've got to go back into hospital. Gideon is telling me to kill myself and Matthew fighting all the time to keep me alive. The torture goes on. What should I do?"

KEYWORKER:   "Maybe you need to go into hospital to feel safe?"

## Analysis

I don't think we can fully estimate or appreciate the force and magnitude of the "mad self" to drive the patient to be destructive to himself and others. This patient has been able to name his "mad self", Gideon, which in biblical terms means "destroyer", "mighty warrior", or "feller of trees". Having been face to face with the "mad self" many times, in psychiatric hospitals, secure units, prisons, outpatient and private patient settings, and also in management and leadership (Kapur, 2009 and Chapter Eight of this text), I can only but conclude that the forcefulness of this "mad self" as a "feller of people" can never be underestimated. For this and many patients, to live with such a state of mind that internally generates such destructive forces (as compared with the external forces described above) must be a source of extreme discomfort, but perversely (as in Bion's original four point description of the psychotic personality) also a source of pleasure in its sadistic intentions. As was the case with this and many other patients, it is so difficult to contain the wish to collapse or retaliate in the face of such hostile provocation. Referring to Chapter One, I think this is where containment is a crucial concept in trying to establish a therapeutic atmosphere. "Rolling with the punches" and/or "experiencing the despair/deadness" of the other person and then trying to put into words the patient's state of mind is a skilful and thankless task. However, if the professional/staff member can demonstrate this commitment to the patient, then there may be the chance of some easement of the "internal Gideon" that is hell-bent on destructiveness. With this in mind, an alternative comment could be:

> "When Gideon takes over, there is no stopping the bad feelings that take over and of course, you worry that you could harm me. However, I think you know I and Matthew (a close friend who died several years ago) can support you to help keep you alive."

This "mapping" interpretation takes account of the preliminary and tentative doctoral research finding (Kapur, 1998) reported in Chapter Six. However, this is a serious attempt to let the patient know that the keyworker/therapist can understand the "life and death" struggles of the severely disturbed state of mind.

More recently, Sinason and Richards (2014) have refined their thinking by referring to the "mad self" as the "internal other". Their justification for doing so is to avoid the idea that the "mad self" would feel persecuted by its very presence, which in reality has been the identity that has kept the patient functioning, albeit at a destructive/dysfunctional level. In suggesting this refinement from what they had previously called the "co-habitee", they write:

> The two "I's" in the inner world each see themselves as the true "I" and hate the enforced proximity of sharing one body. In our discussions in the psychosis workshop at the Willesden Centre, we likened this to being "forced to live in one room together with another person for the whole of your life". In our first published papers MS and JR referred to the two minds which were forced to live in one body as being two cohabitees of a single body. However, we were disconcerted to find that the term "co-habitee" rapidly became identified solely with the mind that operates in a unilateral, self-sufficient mode. It then started to be used in discussion as if it was a "name" for the internal other in a way that loses sight of the fact that each mind is "self to itself" and "other to the other". It is exactly because of the interchangeable nature of the personal pronoun "I" in the inner world, that it is all too easy to lose your mind and find yourself misidentified with the internal other. In subsequent publications we have, therefore, used the relative terms "other self" and "internal other" to underline the reciprocal nature of the experience of the "otherness" within. (Sinason & Richards, 2014, p. 320)

I think the crucial aspect of this recent thinking is that when putting words to the patient's takeover by the "internal other", we do not blame the patient for feeling the way he feels in relating to us in a self-sufficient, destructive, and superior way. If we can tolerate this takeover, weather the "psychic storm", and convey some understanding, then the "sane/other self" may have an idea that depending on us for help is a worthwhile and helpful task (as long as we are presenting our "sane self" to the patient or in Kleinian terminology, depressive position functioning (Brenman, 2006)).

In concluding their recent paper and referring to the case of Mrs. B., Sinason and Richards write:

> By using the framework of internal cohabitation both therapist and patient came to understand that the opposition to the analytic work was being carried out by the internal other in a desperate attempt to save that self's life. Opposition to the analytic work was previously seen as sabotage by the patient of her own progress and that she had to recognise and own this. Such an understanding did not do justice to Mrs. B. or to the fixity, concretism and paranoia of the belief in self-sufficiency that governs the mind of the internal other. (2014, p. 325)

# CHAPTER FIVE

# Training

As will be described later in Chapter Seven on "Consultancy and External Expertise", the provision of training is very much determined by the particular characteristics of the organisation delivering a service. For example, when I worked in the NHS it was accepted that the only staff that could work directly with patients were those qualified in psychiatry or social care (psychiatrists, clinical psychologists, psychiatric nurses, social workers, and occupational therapists). In contrast, within the voluntary and housing sector you can have staff with no vocational qualifications working with the most mentally ill patients and thus being poorly equipped to deal with the day-to-day management of such patients (O'Neill & Wells, 2015). An anomaly in the provision of services for mental illness is that a patient can leave a ward staffed with highly qualified mental and health professionals and move the same day to a residential/supported living setting, with few staff being aware of the breadth and depth of expertise required to provide the best support and care for the very same patient.

In this chapter, I will start from where I was in Threshold, twenty-five years ago, as a senior clinical psychologist who had just left the NHS, having completed my own psychoanalytic experience based on the tripartite training model of personal therapy/analysis, supervision of individual patients, and understanding of the theoretical/knowledge base of the model, which I found most helpful in working with severely mentally ill patients. Figure 2 describes this training model I adopted after making the mistake of assuming newly employed staff with no vocational qualifications could jump to the top of "Maslow's Hierarchy" without having their foundations anchored in the basic requirements of mental health and social care.

Before I consider the five levels of the training hierarchy as they apply to creating therapeutic atmospheres for people with severe mental illness, I will comment on what is the best way to learn, or be trained in a way that enhances knowledge and thus expertise and skills. I will refer to a recent academic text (McKee & Eraut, 2012) and also the psychoanalytic theory relied upon in this book. Eraut (2012) cites the desirable attributes of microclimates for learning in the workplace as:

- A blame-free culture which provides support.
- Learning from experiences, positive and negative, at both group and individual levels.
- Encouraging and talking about learning.
- Trying to make full use of the knowledge resources of its members from outside the group.

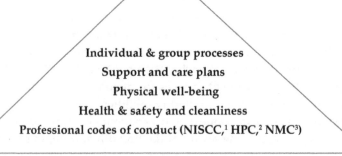

Figure 2. Maslow's training hierarchy.
[1] Northern Ireland Social Care Council.
[2] Health & Care Professions Council.
[3] Nursing & Midwifery Council.

– Enhancing and extending understandings and capabilities of both the group as a whole and its individual members. (p. 27)

This approach is often combined with reflective practice (Schon, 1983). This is an idea that emerged from Dewey's (1933) notion of "reflection on experience" which points to a learning loop from something that appears as a problem, to thinking about solutions to be tested out, to ideas to solve the problem, using potentially a "living learning" experience whereby new knowledge and expertise becomes embedded in the work of the individual/professional staff member. However, in my previous role as training co-ordinator in Threshold and course director of a postgraduate/qualification training in psychoanalytic psychotherapy from 1999–2004, I have not found this model to be entirely successful. What I found is that, particularly in the fields of mental health, social care, and psychoanalytic psychotherapy, there are individuals who are embedded in a "learning through books pattern" which colludes with "paranoid-schizoid" functioning and leaves the patient facing an emotionally distant, superior worker/professional/psychotherapist. I think this is best captured by the title of Bion's (1962) book *Learning from Experience*. Lopez-Corvo (2003) comments on this:

> He (Bion) discriminates between a form of "learning from experience" that changes the learner, and "learning something" that might increase information, but does not change the individual. He refers to the hatred of "learning from experience", which represents the feeling that "experience" is not necessary for learning, because it can be achieved suddenly, as if it were by magic. (p. 163)

Whether it is, as per Figure 2.

– Learning that a code of conduct matters.
– Keeping vulnerable patients safe and in a clean environment.
– Helping severely mentally ill patients keep physically well.
– Providing effective support and care plans.
– Putting words to the most urgent atmosphere in an individual or group setting.

The person receiving the learning has to be in the "depressive position" to take on board the implications of what he reflects upon. Otherwise, an intellectual and limited engagement will occur that will only lead to the patient receiving impoverished and limited help. The likelihood of being treated as a part-object is high.

This, of course, is difficult to control and in my experience as a trainer, you are very much at the mercy of the individual responsibility and ethical standards of the employee/student/trainee, as well as how much that individual functions in the paranoid-schizoid/depressive position. However, the following can be a good guide as to the definition of competence:

> ... being able to perform the tasks and roles required to the expected standard. This expectation, being socially defined, will either be part of professional regulation or be determined by the micropolitics of the particular context. (McKee & Eraut, 2012, pp. 3–4)

This brings us to the first level of Figure 2 professional conduct or standards. I will refer to my own profession's standards of conduct (Health & Care Professions Council, 2008) and the Northern Ireland Social Care Council's code of conduct (NISCC, 2002) to highlight the basic requirement in mental health and social care. While the psychotherapy bodies (UKCP and BCP) have their own voluntary codes, I will rely mainly on HPC and NISCC as they inform the practice of staff in most mental health and social care settings.

The idea of a code is to set standards whereby staff can benchmark their practice to the set standard. HPC has fourteen standards, which are:

1. You must act in the best interests of service users.
2. You must respect the confidentiality of service users.
3. You must keep high standards of personal conduct.
4. You must provide any important information about your conduct and competence.
5. You must keep your professional knowledge up to date.
6. You must act within the limits of your knowledge, skills, and experience, and, if necessary, refer the matter to another practitioner.
7. You must communicate properly and effectively with service users and other practitioners.
8. You must effectively supervise tasks that you have asked other people to carry out.

9. You must get informed consent to give treatment (except in an emergency).
10. You must keep accurate records.
11. You must deal fairly and safely with the risks of infection.
12. You must limit your work or stop practising if your performance or judgement is affected by your health.
13. You must behave with honesty and integrity and make sure that your behaviour does not damage the public's confidence in you or your profession.
14. You must make sure that any advertising you do is accurate.

NISCC has six standards:

1. As a social care worker, you must protect the rights and promote the interests of service users and carers.
2. As a social care worker, you must strive to establish and maintain the trust and confidence of service users and carers.
3. As a social care worker, you must promote the independence of service users while protecting them as far as possible from danger or harm.
4. As a social care worker, you must respect the rights of service users while seeking to ensure that their behaviour does not harm themselves or other people.
5. As a social care worker, you must uphold public trust and confidence in social care services.
6. As a social care worker, you must be accountable for the quality of your work and take responsibility for maintaining and improving your knowledge and skills.

I think there are three main themes throughout both of these codes of conduct:

− As in the medical dictum, "Do no harm".
− Boundaries are essential; know what you do well and work within your limitations.
− Continue lifelong learning, in whatever form that may take.

In the real world of mental health and care (and healthcare, as indicated by the Francis Report, 2013), adherence to these standards is random and dependent on the values of each individual professional. For example, in my own profession, there is considerable controversy as to the need for personal therapy/analysis, either during or after professional qualification. In contrast, in traditional psychoanalytic training, it would be deemed immoral/unprofessional to analyse patients without you yourself being analysed. Of course the depth and breadth of analytic work is determined by the theoretical modes and style of the training analyst/therapist. In the theoretical model adopted in this text, the value base is clear, as highlighted by Rosenfeld (1987) in his work with psychotic patients:

> As I have mentioned in description of my own development, contact with one's hidden psychotic areas is an essential part of being in touch with the patient and the psychotic transference relationship. Such anxieties must become activated during the treatment of psychotic patients but, if they are not thoroughly dealt with through personal psychoanalysis, it can create confusion and impasse in the therapy as well as severe strain and even disaster for the therapist. The psychotic patient often projects his feelings and problems quite violently and any analyst who is afraid of such contact with his patient might himself become severely disturbed in attempting to treat psychosis. The most frequent but often unconscious anxiety is the fear of being driven mad by the patient. It is for this reason that the analysis of the analyst should be particularly thorough, and this of course includes the experience of the psychotic areas of the analyst, so that the psychotic anxieties and defences can be worked through sufficiently during the training period ... only in this way can he respond to the patient with empathy without too much involvement and also show sensitivity and receptiveness without being overwhelmed by the patient's projection. (pp. 18–19)

What I am trying to illustrate here is that the value base of the individual staff member/professional will drive adherence to the standards of conduct and determine the depth and breadth to which these are met. For the staff member, I, as an employer, as a CEO, have lines of accountability and management that allow me to monitor and control adherence to these standards. However, in psychoanalytic parlance, if the psychotic (destructive) personality of the staff member/professional feels she or he knows best then it is near impossible to stop a critical incident affecting the patient. What I have found most helpful is establishing a training culture (Kapur, 2008b) which maximises the opportunity for staff to learn and thus minimise the chance of individuals doing their own (psychotic) thing. This, combined with firm lines of accountability (which are not present in private psychotherapy practice) helps minimise the risk of harm to the patient.

As stated in Chapter Two, establishing the basic aspects of good rehabilitative care is essential to ensure that the physical and social needs of the patient are met. Often, in the world of therapeutic approaches in looking after the needs of severely mentally ill patients, the fundamental needs of patient care are neglected. For example, in residential care, food hygiene, fire safety, and first aid training are essential for staff to create a safe environment. It is tempting for staff to neglect these aspects of patient care in favour of the talking therapies as they see the former "something I shouldn't have to do". However, I have found in training staff, if they neglect these fundamentals of patient care then they are less likely to think and talk about patients in a comprehensive way, whereby *all* the patients' needs are met.

Figure 2 points to the importance of addressing the physical needs of patients.

Poor physical health has been correlated with people with severe mental illness. Harris & Barraclough (1998) found that more than twenty-seven forms of mental disorder were linked to an increased risk of premature death, with over 60% due to natural causes. They suggest this is due to the effects of mental illness and the patient's altered lifestyle. Brown, Barraclough, and Inskip (2000) noted the excess mortality rate for those suffering from schizophrenia over patients with diseases of the circulatory, respiratory, digestive, endocrine, and nervous systems. So it is crucial, as we progress up the training hierarchy, that staff are equipped with the expertise to be aware of the needs of the severely mentally ill patient.

Chapter Two also highlights the importance of care and support plans, providing an individualised approach to making sure all the needs of the patient are met. It is crucial that staff are trained in how to design and implement such plans, particularly for those staff who are not trained in the core mental health professions.

Finally, at the top of the hierarchy and what is the added ingredient in a mental health and social care setting that creates a therapeutic atmosphere, is the training of staff in the group processes (Chapter Three) and individual understanding of patients (Chapter Four). I think this is where Eraut's (2012) concept of a "microclimate" is particularly helpful. This is not unlike the training atmospheres I found when I undertook my supervision of cases in a group setting. The capacity to think about the patient is maximised in a non-persecutory environment and all contributions are welcome to help understand the emotional life of the patient, whether that is in an individual or group setting. Case discussion, when complemented by theoretical understanding, can provide a powerful way of equipping staff with the knowledge and expertise to create an atmosphere where the patient feels understood and accepted and thus potentially eases the emotional effects of severe mental illness.

# CHAPTER SIX

# Research

Applying research findings in the real world of mental health and social care is rare. It is unusual for staff to be aware of the relevant and most recent findings from psychotherapy research in constructing the most beneficial therapeutic community/ environment/atmosphere as well as being aware of the best research-driven guidelines as to how to speak to a patient as an individual and to groups. Often staff are applying theoretically driven ideas only (particularly in the case of psychoanalytic interventions) or are relying on anecdotal accounts of what they believe works best. What I will do in this chapter is review the relevant research in creating therapeutic atmospheres (including therapeutic communities) through individual and group therapeutic interventions as they apply to working with people with severe mental illness. For individual and group interventions, I will offer a RIG (research informed guideline) which professionals can keep in mind when constructing a therapeutic atmosphere, conducting a small or large group, or speaking individually to people with severe mental illness.

## Therapeutic atmosphere

One of the very first studies looking at the ingredients of a helpful and effective therapeutic atmosphere was by Vaglum, Friis, and Karterud (1985), working with psychotic patients in short-term and intermediate wards. They found that confronting group therapy is detrimental and an individually orientated link is helpful. Large groups were not particularly effective. They also found that a large number of psychotic patients clustered in a ward was not helpful, with a huge turnover of staff leading to a detrimental atmosphere. Importantly, they found when they intervened and made groups more talk-orientated, or when they increased the amount of individual therapy and reduced the number of beds, the ward atmosphere improved considerably.

RIG:   **Confrontation is not effective. Individual work with a limited number of patients works best.**

A relevant paper by Karterud (1988a) points to the adoption of the particular therapeutic community model as outlined in Chapter Two, as relevant mainly for patients in long-term settings, with a personality disorder or severe neuroses. Using his own "Group Emotionality Rating System" and "Group Focal Conflict Analysis" measures, he captured Bion's basic assumption functioning in a therapeutic community and short-term wards. He found that extreme fight/flight groups occurred mostly in short-term wards adopting a therapeutic community model.

RIG:   **Therapeutic community models are not helpful for the multiplicity of emergency cases in a short-term psychiatric ward.**

A piece of research that captured basic assumption functioning across different patient populations is Karterud's (1988b) paper exploring the prevalence of these behaviours with personality disorders, psychosis, and major depression. The Group Emotionality Rating System was applied to approximately 1700 verbal statements from ninety-one patients in seventy-five small group therapy sessions. Patients with personality disorders demonstrated the strongest values for fight/flight while patients with major depression showed the strongest values for dependency. Patients with neurosis and personality disorder scored higher for pairing than patients with psychoses. Some modification of this basic assumption functioning did seem to occur in a structured group therapy culture.

RIG:    **Personality disordered patients fight/flight most and pair (along with neurotic patients) more than psychotic patients. Depressed patients are the most dependent on the group leader.**

In reviewing the research literature on therapeutic atmospheres, the work of Rudolf Moos (1996a, 1996b, 1997) is relevant to capture key ingredients of what is most helpful in a setting for severely mentally ill patients. Using a measure that he calls the "Community Orientated Programmes Environment Scale" (COPES) derived from his "Ward Atmosphere Scale" (WAS), Moos (1997) identified some general relationships between aspects of the treatment environment and patients in programme outcomes. Generally, he found that when patients felt supported and were allowed to direct themselves and felt "understood", then they were more satisfied with treatment. Patients in a well organised setting with clear programmes tended to do well. Also, when patients were more involved/engaged in programmes, they then felt more attached, revealed more, and were able to express more negative feelings. Conversely, high staff control was inhibiting and was associated with low patient morale/self-confidence, less openness, and more negativity towards staff. Where therapeutic programmes lacked focus there emerged high drop-out rates.

In adding to the above research findings, Timko and Moos (1998) compared treatment climates and in-programme patient profiles across two settings. Overall, they found that a programme characterised by high resident input, policy clarity, and focus, scored higher on patients feeling supported, practically engaged, and autonomous, and had a capacity to solve problems, compared to a programme with less resident input and policy clarity.

RIG:    **Therapeutic atmospheres that are well organised, promote patient engagement, and have an ordered optimal staff input seem to be the most helpful.**

## Groups

Most of the findings to be reported below refer to formal group psychotherapy. In this arrangement, there are usually one or two group leaders, with an average group size of between six and eight, meeting once weekly for between an hour and an hour and a half. The group is either open-ended over several years or within a closed time frame (say ten weeks). However, these guidelines are equally applicable and helpful when speaking to patients with severe mental illness in small or larger groups without the above specifications.

Most of the following research to be cited has previously been reviewed by myself (Kapur, 1999). What I will do here, as previously in this chapter, is point to the content of each piece of research and recommend particular RIGs.

It was Sigmund Karterud (1989) who was one of the first psychotherapy researchers to explore the effect of different therapeutic styles on patients suffering from psychotic disorders in inpatient settings. He explored the effects of the following interventions: promoting interaction, clarification, confrontation, interpretation, giving advice and suggestions, technical neutrality, and managing boundaries issues. He compared three therapeutic community environments that he termed TC1, TC2, and TC3. TC1 had a typical therapeutic community setting in a ward with just under 50 per cent suffering from psychoses. TC2 and TC3 occurred in the community settings with TC2 having only 27 per cent of its patients suffering from a psychotic illness, compared to 58 per cent in TC3. Across these three settings, all patients were randomly assigned to small therapy groups. Using the Group Emotionality Rating Scale (GERS) (previously cited in this chapter) he measured Bion's basic assumption functioning. He found TC2 exhibited less fight/flight behaviour than TC1 and TC3. In particular, TC1's overtly confrontational groups led to more fight/flight behaviour.

RIG:   **Effective group functioning is enhanced by non-confrontational interventions.**

In exploring the effects of specific interventions, my own research (Kapur, 1993) explored the immediate impact of group interpretations with severely mentally ill patients. In this "Bion style" interpretation, the focus is on putting into words the emotional atmosphere in the group, particularly in relation to the group leader. Seven elements of interpretive activity were studied. These were: accuracy, transference (interpretations in relation to the group leader), bridge-making (links between clinical material and inferred meanings), clarity, group focus (here the interpretation addressed the group as a whole), immediacy, and empathy.

In referring to Bion's concept of "attacks on linking" (see Chapter One), it was suggested that if the group leader was accurate in his here and now transferential interpretations, then these would be a negative response. In contrast, it was suggested the other four elements would elicit a good response. The data was collected in acute inpatient settings with small groups of mainly psychotic patients. A correlation (multiple regression) analysis revealed that there was some evidence that high transference-orientated interpretations are slightly associated with low patient responsiveness and vice versa.

Clinically, this is an interesting finding. If we adopt the theoretical model described in Chapter One, then this "attack on linking" is inevitable, but if worked through could establish purposeful links with the group leader, as these links are proposed to be essential for mental and physical growth (Bion, 1959; Grinberg, Sor, & Debianchedi, 1975). However, from a Foulkesian and Yalom-based perspective (see Chapter Three), these interventions would not be seen as helpful for the patient.

RIG: **"In transference" interpretations may elicit less patient responsiveness, but (theoretically) may be helpful for the patient.**

In adopting an interactive psychodynamic approach to outpatient work with chronic psychotic patients, Profita, Correy, and Klein (1989) evaluated the effects of such an intervention. A major limitation of this study was the failure to accurately describe the theoretical basis of their technique, referring to it generally as a mixture of interpretative and interpersonal interventions. Twelve patients were involved in the study and all suffered from a mixture of chronic schizophrenia and depression. These researchers used a combination of their own objective (frequency of re-hospitalisations) and subjective (capacity to comply with treatment recommendations and acquisition of independent living skills) measures of change and found that having the same group therapist conduct the sessions was important, eliciting positive change. Unfortunately they make no empirical link between process and outcome and thus their findings are limited.

RIG: **Group therapist/leader, continuity, reliability, and stability are associated with a good outcome.**

There has been a considerable amount of research on therapeutic factors in inpatient groups working with severely mentally ill patients, for example, Betcher (1983); Brabender (1985); Budman (1981); Cory and Page (1978); R. H. Klein (1977); Leszcz, Yalom, and Norden (1988); Marcovitz and Smith (1983); Pekala, Siegal, and Ferrar (1985); Waxer (1977); Yalom (1983);. All of this research, along with my own findings (Kapur, Miller, & Mitchell, 1988; Kapur, Ramage, & Waller, 1986) and research by Pappas, Yannitsi, and Liakos (1997) suggests that the therapeutic factors of cohesiveness, universality, and learning from interpersonal actions are the most important. Most of these groups adopted a structured, "turn-taking" approach (Yalom, 1983), where there was a clear agenda set for the group and under the direction of the group leader(s), severely mentally ill patients were given an opportunity to engage in specific issues raised, whether that was around decreasing isolation, alleviating hospital-related anxiety, engaging the patient in the therapeutic process, or other similar themes relating to the experience of being a psychiatric patient in a ward (Yalom & Leszc, 2005).

RIG:    **In a structured group, severely mentally ill patients find being part of a group, sharing similar difficulties, and learning from others, to be most helpful.**

One of the most difficult and controversial issues facing the group therapist conducting a group of psychotic patients is whether to adopt a structured approach to minimise the psychotic anxieties of the patient (Yalom, 1983) or to allow such anxieties to emerge, whereby patients can introject more positive experiences and so negate the primitive internal object relations which so quickly manifest with disturbed states of mind (as described in Chapter One). There are many clinical arguments for and against structured and unstructured approaches. In a nutshell, the argument focuses on whether therapists are exposing patients to unnecessary frustration and pain by not directing events or whether the eruption of primitive anxieties within such groups has a detoxifying effect (Pines, 2000), where patients are "relieved" of carrying such internal pressures. Green and Cole (1991) explore this question by investigating the effects of structured and unstructured groups with severely mentally ill patients, using a theoretical model based on the work of Kernberg (1976).

The findings of their study broadly support their clinical view that psychotic patients prefer structured groups while they found borderline patients prefer unstructured groups. While Greene and Cole (1991) speculate on the theoretical constructs which explain these findings, they do not consider the alternative hypotheses of psychosis exhibiting a negative therapeutic reaction to unstructured groups, as described in Chapter One, which if worked through could result in the introjection/ internalisation of psychic structures that could lead to positive change. Clinically, in inpatient settings, it seems appropriate to follow clinical wisdom where a structured group for psychotic patients may be most helpful. However, in long-term group psychotherapy with psychotic patients, the research question has still to be answered as to whether containment of psychotic anxieties could lead to a successful outcome.

RIG:    **In inpatient settings, psychotic patients may be most helped by structured group therapy.**

Opalic (1989) investigated the effects of group psychotherapy with neurotic and psychotic patients, compared a treatment group with small group therapy with a co-treatment group consisting of psychiatric check-ups only. He found that for both patient populations, the patient's experience of being understood by others was conducive to a favourable experience. In particular, psychotic patients seemed to feel that group psychotherapy allowed them to speak more freely of their own views; there was also a value in verbalising the entire range of emotional and sensual life experiences of group members, which may have been previously inhibited. Opalic (1989) also found that the experience of the group gave psychotic patients a strong feeling of being accepted, particularly in the expression of feelings of "love and hate".

RIG:    **Psychiatric patients can benefit from feeling understood by others in groups, as well as having opportunities to express the whole spectrum of feelings from love to hate.**

Finally, Lefevre (1994) measured the power of countertransference in groups for severely mentally ill patients. Small groups were conducted in a large mental hospital with the researcher using a definition of countertransference consistent with this text (Heimann, 1950). These responses of the patients were measured by asking the facilitators to record their feelings in terms of frequency, powerfulness, and importance immediately after the groups. The ten most common feelings were empathy, frustration, achievement, exhaustion, feeling shattered, anxiety, sadness, happiness, hopelessness, and emptiness. While this is a simple study with no clear empirical methodology, it does highlight the emotional pressure on the container of the staff member/group leader in working with such patients and the importance of support.

RIG: **When working with psychotic patients, ensure there is a full support framework, preferably including supervision and personal therapy/analysis.**

## Outcome measures

While outcome measures represent the mantra of evidence-based approaches, few clinicians are aware of the huge limitations of outcome research in the real world of mental health and social care. This not only refers to the motivation of organisations and staff to complete evaluation measures but it also refers to the complexity and, at times, impossibility of capturing the multidimensional mixture of outcomes (Schaffer, 1982). What I will do here is review the main issues in selecting an outcome measure and then suggest several clinically relevant measurements. I think the important data that can realistically be collected follows the medical dictum of "doing no harm" from pre-test/ treatment and post-test/treatment evaluations. Cause and effect relationships (as I will describe below) cannot be proven and only a small, albeit important dimension of overall outcomes can be captured.

### Quasi-experimental designs

It was the original work of Cook and Campbell (1979) which distinguished between four types of validity that permit conclusions to be drawn between process (independent) and outcome (dependent) variables. In other words, depending on the type of study and how much we can control the treatment intervention, what "safe" conclusions can we draw from what we do and what the outcome is?

I will review these four aspects of validity with particular reference to conducting a simple pre- and post-intervention study, as this will be the most likely evaluation of outcomes in the real world of mental health and social care. The findings I will present later in this chapter will cite Threshold's "real world" study which is of this design.

## Statistical conclusion validity

For many clinicians and particularly psychoanalytic psychotherapists, the issue of statistics tends to unnecessarily confuse and create a barrier to taking part in and conducting any research. While this is understandable, most studies do rely on the advice of an expert statistician to ensure the accuracy of conclusions that are drawn. In the use of statistical conclusion validity, the issue of how the numbers that are gathered from the measures are collected and analysed, dictates how we might say that a particular treatment has a significant effect.

One of the major issues that affects whether we can say a treatment has a particular effect is to do with "statistical power", which is dictated by the size of the sample. A small sample will often not be able to generate enough such power to differentiate between a treatment having no or any effect. Here a statistician will apply a statistical power test to the sample to determine the magnitude of any change (see Threshold study cited later).

## Internal validity

How a treatment is delivered constitutes the second threat to the conclusions that can be drawn between what is done (process) and its effect (outcome). This is at the heart of quantitative research studies, the empirical proof of a cause and effect relationship, in other words, "Does X cause Y?" Scientific studies that present this evidence are scarce in psychological research as it is difficult to establish the "gold standard" of a RCT (randomised controlled trial) in the real world of psychotherapy, particularly psychoanalytic psychotherapy. In many ways this is a direct contradiction of the discussions that take place in psychoanalytic work, where there are so many assumptions that X causes Y, for instance, holiday breaks upsetting the patient. However, for the purposes of understanding research, we can see that there is often an inverse relationship between internal validity and external validity (application of findings to the real world). It is not unlike a "see-saw" relationship, as "one goes up, the other comes down". So in the field of psychotherapy research, it is difficult to explore real clinical events and establish an empirical cause and effect relationship, which really can only be achieved by an RCT. Nevertheless, what is possible (as has been demonstrated by psychotherapy research findings cited in this chapter) is to present findings within the limitations of stipulating cause and effect, according to the original hierarchy of evidence of Sackett, Rosenberg, Groy, Hernes, and Richardson (1996). This means that we are cautious, suggestive rather than definitive about the interpretations we apply to our findings. Often this appears as "correlational data", say that X correlates with Y, suggesting "something is happening" in the process which affects the outcome. Such tentativeness I think is a hallmark of good psychoanalytic clinical practice.

## Construct validity

This refers to how adequately we can capture the treatment under investigation as, particularly in the psychoanalytic therapies, it is multifaceted. For example, if we are suggesting interpretation has a specific effect, can we assume that the same "construct" called interpretation is being applied consistently about treatment interventions we may be investigating. A similar problem is that of "non-specific" effects first identified by Strupp (1970), where issues of hope and expectation may outweigh the specificity of any intervention. Third, there is the problem of investigator bias, of "seeing what we really want to see" and observing cause and effect relationships when they are not really there. Related to this is the problem of bias on self-report or therapist rated outcomes, where the patient or therapist may be rating towards their own predetermined judgements, rather than capturing an objective measure of the patient's functioning under investigation. Fifth, outcome measures are multidimensional (Schaffer, 1982) and, therefore, in reporting any finding, we have to be careful to stipulate the limitations of our findings as rarely can we be multidimensional in measuring behaviour, thoughts, and feelings from three possible sources (therapist, patient, and significant other). I do think that in current mantra based interventions, this important issue has been "swept under the carpet" to make claims on psychological change that simply cannot be proven, for example, the assumption that CBT effects deeper psychological change is simply that; it may be that outcome measures capturing emotional states of mind indicate that the patient is deteriorating. A final aspect of construct validity refers to the timing of outcome assessment. Where possible, follow-up outcome data can prevent findings being given greater weight than the true effect over the time period of the intervention.

## External validity

As stated above, external validity is the strength of psychoanalytic work as it works within the "real world" of the therapist/patient interaction. However, in these uncontrolled conditions, it is impossible to establish strong internal validity (cause and effect) as we are exploring the spontaneous events of a psychotherapy session. However, research to be reported later (Kapur, 1993, 1998) does offer an example of how this can be done, within the limitations of this research not being able to control both process (treatment) and its effect on outcome.

## Macro-outcome findings

As stated above, in selecting any outcome measure, we have to be careful in interpreting our findings in the context of:

- Naturalistic studies in the real world of mental health and social care are not RCTs and thus cannot provide any evidence of "cause and effect".
- All outcome measures are limited in the dimensions of the individual functioning they capture and the source of this information.

Within Threshold, we have explored many different outcome measures. Our original evaluation (Kapur et al., 1997) will be reported first, followed by our recent outcome findings (unpublished).

This initial evaluation used three measures to capture outcome:

- Global Assessment Scale (GAS, Endicott, Spitzer, Fleiss, & Cohen, 1976), which is a staff rated measure attempting to capture the patients' psychological and psychiatric functioning between zero and 100. The lower end of the scale indicates poor functioning such as "needs constant supervision for several days to prevent hurting self or others or to maintain personal hygiene". Mid-point on the scale (50 points) indicates moderate functioning such as "any serious symptomatology or impairment in functioning that most clinicians would think obviously requires treatment or attention" (e.g., suicidal gesture, frequent anxiety attacks). The top end of the scale (100) represents "superior functioning in a wide range of activities; life's problems never seem to get out of hand".

- Brief Psychiatric Rating Scale (BPRS), which is a popular measure used in psychiatric settings (Overall & Gorham, 1962) where staff assess levels of anxiety and depression as well as psychotic symptomatology.
- Therapeutic Community Questionnaire (TCQ) developed by Wagenborg, Tremeronti, Hesselink, and Koning (1988), which is a self-report measure designed to capture how the patient "thinks and feels" about himself and others.

All three measures have strong reliability and validity features, so ensuring they can capture accurately the areas of function they are focusing on.

Our results found that with twenty-two of the thirty-five patients (61 per cent that remained in the therapeutic community over eighteen months, 80 per cent of whom suffered from a psychotic disorder, 51 per cent were female and 49 per cent male), there were:

- Significant improvements in their "blunted effect", defined as "reduced emotional tone and apparent lack of normal feeling and involvement", and "unco-operativeness", defined as "evidence of resistance, unfriendliness, resentment".
- In the overall GAS scores, there was a small but significant movement from "serious" to "moderate" symptomatology and problems.
- In the TCQ, patients reported that the longer they stayed within the therapeutic community, the lower they perceived the severity of the problem on their admission. It seems that retrospectively, patients felt more positive about the effects of previous treatments.

Overall, this initial study with a small sample (and thus limited statistical power) tentatively indicates that patients were more engaged and seemed to improve after a short period of time with us. At the very least, we can suggest that something helpful seems to have occurred in the therapeutic community setting which seems to have helped these patients with severe mental illness.

Our most recent evaluation adopted the "Wisconsin Quality of Life" (WQL) self-report measure to capture the overall quality of functioning with severely mentally ill patients. We felt that this outcome could capture the features of psychiatric rehabilitation that was more relevant from a patient moving out of the hospital and into the community.

*Wisconsin quality of life mental health index (WQL-MHI)*

While Threshold operates a therapeutic approach/model to its work with severely mentally ill patients, it is important to remember that we work within the real world of mental health and social care and thus our patients will exhibit all the traditional signs, symptoms, and psychopathology of a typical psychiatric patient. It is with this in mind that we selected the above measure (Becker, Diamond, & Sainfort, 1993; Diamond & Becker, 1999).

The measure is an easy to use, self-administered questionnaire which assesses nine separate domains that together encompass the quality of life. These are:

1. **Satisfaction level**: This general measure of life satisfaction covers a broad range of issues and refers to such things as the client's satisfaction with the living environment, housing, amount of fun, food, clothing, and mental health services. It covers the basic needs in "Maslow's Hierarchy" with each indicator rated on an ordinal scale (ordered scale with no assumption of an agreed baseline) ranging from "very dissatisfied" to "very satisfied". Each indicator is also rated for importance on a scale ranging from "not at all important" to "extremely important". The score for each item is determined by multiplying each patient's satisfaction response with the importance response. The index also includes a global question for rating feeling about life as a whole on a seven point scale from one (very unhappy) to seven (very happy).

2. **Occupational attitudes**: Six questions are devoted to the patient's work, school, or day programming, such as, "Do you feel you are working or are in school, less than you would like, as much as you would like, more than you would like?"

3. **Psychological well-being**: This domain attempts to measure the subjective well-being of the patient. The researchers (Becker, Diamond, & Sainfort, 1993) include the Bradburn Affect Balance Scale (Ryff, 1989) which assesses both negative and positive affects. The patient is also asked to rate his mental health on a scale ranging from poor to excellent and how he feels about his overall subjective feeling of well-being.

4. **Physical health**: Here the patient is asked about his perception of his physical health. He is asked to rate physical health on a five-point

scale from poor to excellent (very dissatisfied to very satisfied) as to how important physical health is to him (not at all important to extremely important).

5. **Activities of daily living (ADL):** The WQL-MHI incorporates the entire life skills profile (LSP) developed by Rosen, Hadzi-Povlowic, and Parker (1989), which was tested in a large sample of subjects with schizophrenia. Also the researchers incorporated a scale developed by Spitzer et al. (1981) which has five questions capturing the patient's engagement with ordinary activities, such as going for a walk.

6. **Social relationships:** In this measure, social relationships are defined as active participation with others. Questions are also included regarding activities that take place in a social context but may or may not represent social relatedness (e.g., going to the cinema or participating in sport). This domain originates from earlier research (Breier & Strauss, 1987) which captured the frequency and type of social contact of patients recovering from psychosis in the original International Pilot Study of Schizophrenia (IPSS). Additionally, this domain captures how the patient experiences the social event (amount of support experienced and perceived satisfaction).

7. **Economics:** Questions in this domain ask about the adequacy of a patient's financial support and satisfaction with/importance of the amount of money the patient has. This provides some indication of the socio-economic status of the patient.

8. **Symptoms:** This domain incorporates the Brief Psychiatric Rating Scale (BPRS) previously used in evaluating Threshold's services (see above).

9. **Goals for improvement with treatment:** The patient is asked to specify the three most important goals for his improvement with treatment, using a ten-point rating of how important the goal is to how much has been achieved.

In the scoring, each domain is weighted according to the patient's evaluation of its importance and by re-scaling the items using this "preference". Accurate overall scores are achieved by this procedure which capture the clinical significance (for the patient) of each domain. Thus, in using this measure, we can be reasonably confident that we are capturing the patient's progress, as he assesses it, as a mixture of objective and subjective measures. An overall score is also calculated from all the domains.

## Findings

We have been routinely collecting data for several years, using the WQL-MHI. Tables 3a and 3b contain demographic and diagnostic details of the sample. Table 3c reports the mean scores at baseline (admission) and eighteen months (stay) for 122 patients. As we can see, the original baseline had a sample size of 357, which means that either 235 had not been in our projects for eighteen months or not completed the questionnaire. With so many dropouts in this longitudinal study, a statistical analysis was undertaken using the "last completed" questionnaire as the scores/data point in the analysis. This is an accepted technique in a straightforward, one sample, pre- and post-test study. A paired t-test revealed:

- Significant improvements in four of the eight subscales, namely, general satisfaction, occupation, social relations, and money.
- A significant improvement on the overall summary score.

In other words, we can reasonably conclude that after eighteen months, patients felt that they have a good living environment, are involved in daily occupational activities, related well to others, and are satisfied with the amount of money they have. Overall, patients improve with us after eighteen months.

These findings confirm that we seem to be meeting the basic needs of people with severe mental illness, consistent with the recommendations of the TAP Studies (Leff & Trieman, 2000). It may also be that something is occurring within our "relational atmosphere" at Threshold which improves the capacity of severely mentally ill patients to relate to others. Patients, as part of the housing and welfare system, also feel that they have sufficient money to continue to live life as fully as possible. As a voluntary agency, independent of the National Health Service, this indicates that our financial modelling is successful, not only in ensuring that the agency (as a limited company) pays its bills, meets staff salary commitments, but also that sufficient financial independence is still retained by patients for them to continue their independent living with us.

We can conclude that "something in the Threshold atmosphere" seems to be helping our severely mentally ill patients and that we can be reasonably confident that after eighteen months they will improve and not deteriorate. Thus, we have more than met the mantra/dictum of "doing no harm" with the chance that we have contributed to "doing some good". We cannot empirically conclude what particular ingredient in the "Threshold atmosphere" is linked to good outcome; this is for future research endeavours.

Table 3a. Demographic details of sample.

| Sex | N (%) |
|---|---|
| Female | 46 (38%) |
| Male | 76 (62%) |
| Total | 122 (100%) |
| Marital status | |
| Single (never married) | 82 (67%) |
| Married | 7 (6%) |
| Divorced | 16 (13%) |
| Committed relationship | 2 (2%) |
| Separated | 6 (5%) |
| Spouse deceased | 9 (7%) |
| Total | 122 (100%) |

Table 3b. Diagnostic information.

| | N (%) |
|---|---|
| Schizophrenia | 81 (66%) |
| Bipolar disorder | 8 (7%) |
| Depression | 15 (12%) |
| Eating disorder | 1 (1%) |
| Personality disorder | 4 (3%) |
| Asperger's syndrome | 1 (1%) |
| Missing information | 12 (10%) |
| Total | 122 (100%) |

Table 3c. Wisconsin quality of life scores over time.

| Domain | Baseline Mean (SD) N = 357 | 18 months Mean (SD) N = 122 | T | df | Sig** |
|---|---|---|---|---|---|
| General satisfaction | 0.70 (1.16) | 1.14 (1.07) | −0.35 | 243 | 0.000* |
| Occupation activities | 0.32 (1.77) | 0.86 (1.60) | −0.31 | 248 | 0.002* |
| Psychological well-being | −0.42 (1.42) | −0.01 (1.40) | −1.70 | 246 | 0.089 |
| Symptoms/outlook | 0.99 (1.34) | 1/41 (1.34) | −1.15 | 146 | 0.249 |
| Physical health | −0.53 (1.61) | −0.45 (1.67) | −0.21 | 222 | 0.833 |
| Social relations/support | 0.78 (1.32) | 1.08 (1.30) | −2.21 | 245 | 0.028* |
| Money/economics | 0.96 (1.36) | 1.4 (1.19) | −1.97 | 246 | 0.050* |
| Activities of daily living | 1.47 (1.35) | 1.72 (1.17) | −1/75 | 241 | 0.081 |
| WQL total score | 0.54 (0.97) | 0.88 (0.86) | −2.99 | 211 | 0.003* |

*P < .05.

** Analysis based on last observation carried forward.

Higher scores indicate improvement.

## Other outcome studies

Table 4 lists the main other studies in the area of evaluating therapeutic communities for psychosis. I have also included a recently published psychiatric rehabilitation measure (Killaspy et al., 2013) which while not explicitly capturing the effects of therapeutic communities, does address general issues of a therapeutic milieu.

As you can see from the table, and as stated earlier, different aspects of the multidimensional nature of outcome were selected. Chiesa, Fonagy, and Holmes (2004) explored the effects of treatment programmes in the inpatient therapy programme of the Cassel Hospital in Richmond, Surrey and compared this with a traditional psychiatric hospital model. They also looked at the effects of six months' inpatient psychosocial treatment at the Cassel, followed by eighteen months' outpatient group dynamic psychotherapy and six months of concurrent outreach nursing in the community. As a third group, they examined the effects of standard care for personality disorders within North Devon Healthcare NHS Trust. They found that:

... a specialist inpatient psychosocial approach to personality disorder is significantly more effective over time than standard general psychiatric care in the dimensions of symptom distress, social adaptation and global assessment of outcome. The higher effectiveness rates on these dimensions, compared with those of the control group, confirm the results of previous studies in the UK for similar patient groups. (p. 216)

As such, their research did not reveal any significant findings for people with psychosis.

Table 4.  Evaluation of therapeutic communities.

| Study | Outcome measures |
|---|---|
| Chiesa, Fonagy, & Holmes (2004) | – Symptom Check List SCL—90 = R (Derogatis, 1983)<br>– Social Adjustment Scale (Weissman, 1975)<br>– Global Assessment Scale (Endicott, Spitzer, Fleiss, & Cohen, 1976)<br>– Adult Attachment Interview (George, Kaplan, & Main, 1985)<br>– Client Service Receipt Interview (Beecham & Knapp, 1992) |
| Bola & Mosher (2003) | – Readmission to care (yes/no)<br>– Number and days of readmission<br>– Global Psychopathology Scale (Mosher, Pollin, & Stabenernau, 1971)<br>– Global Improvement Scale (Mosher, Pollin, & Stabenernau, 1971)<br>– Living independently or with peers (yes/no)<br>– Working (none, part time, full time)<br>– Social Functioning Scale (Sokis, 1970) |
| Killaspy et al. (2013) | Quality indicator of rehabilitative care<br>– Living environment<br>– Therapeutic environment<br>– Treatments and interventions<br>– Self-management and autonomy<br>– Social inclusion<br>– Human rights<br>– Recovery based practice |

In contrast, Bola and Mosher (2003) specifically compared residential therapeutic community treatment and minimal use of antipsychotic medication with "usual" hospital treatment for patients with early episode schizophrenia spectrum psychosis. Their treatment model or process is described as follows:

> "Traitement Moral" a humanistic trend in the care and treatment of persons with mental illness, can be traced to Pinel's removing chains from the men in Paris' Bicêtre Hospital in 1797. Following in the humanistic tradition, Soteria incorporated aspects of moral treatment (Brockhoven, 1963), Sullivan's (1962) interpersonal theory and specially designed milieu at Sheppard Pratt Hospital [Baltimore, MD] in the 1920s and the "developmental crisis" notion that growth may be possible from psychosis (Laing, 1967; Menninger, 1959; Perry, 1974). (p. 220)

This "atmosphere" is significantly different to that described in Chapter One. However, as in this current text there was no process measure (e.g., Karterud, 1988b) to empirically confirm the adoption and adherence to the Soteria theoretical model, we can only assume that this "humanistic-interpersonal" model was delivered. Bola and Mosher's study employed a quasi-experimental design with seventy-nine patients in the treatment group and 100 receiving "usual hospital" care. Average age of the subjects was 21.7 years with 64 per cent male and 36 per cent female. Analysis of the outcome measures listed in Table 5 were conducted across other groups at the completion of treatment and point of treatment, at the last post-discharge observation, and for those subjects who partially completed the treatment. Those at the end of a partially completed treatment intervention and completion of treatment had significantly better outcomes than the "usual hospital" treatment group, particularly in the areas of psychopathology, work, and social functioning. These were small to medium size effect benefits. They conclude:

> On the whole, these data argue that a relationally focused therapeutic milieu with minimal use of anti-psychotic drugs, rather than drug treatment in the hospital, should be a preferred treatment for persons newly diagnosed with schizophrenia spectrum disorder. (p. 226)

The recent "Quality Indicator of Rehabilitative Care" (QUIRC) covers the seven dimensions listed in Table 5. The measure demonstrated good inter-rater reliability and internal validity, so being able to accurately capture the dimensions listed. What is of particular interest, and may be an accurate measure of therapeutic atmospheres is the measure of therapeutic milieu and recovery-based practices which cover the level of patient involvement and promotion of independent living, and how well staff are engaging with patients. Interestingly, and while not specifically adopting a therapeutic model of rehabilitation, they found one of the strongest influences on outcome was therapeutic environment. In other words, where patients were actively engaged in their promotion of independence, there emerged an association with good outcomes, defined as patient autonomy. Also they found that service quality, as defined by the dimensions of the QUIRC, were not associated with changes in quality of life.

## Outcome measures capturing the "internal world"

While there are psychometric measures that do capture emotional states, such as Plutchik's Emotional Profile Index (Plutchik, 2000; Plutchik & Kellerman, 1974) there are only two measures that specifically aim to capture the internal and deeper emotional life of the patient as described in Chapter One of this text.

## Personal relatedness profile

As described earlier, this particular measure (Hobson, Patrick, & Valentine, 1998) does address interpersonal and intrapsychic processes. In particular, this measure could address any changes that occur in how the patient deeply "thinks and feels" about himself and others. Hobson and colleagues found satisfactory inter-rater reliability in judgements using independent raters on the dimensions of paranoid-schizoid and depressive position functioning, as well as evidence that items were interrelated (see original paper for further psychometric properties). However, in applying this theoretical model, which has been derived from formal and intensive psychoanalysis (patients seen between three and five times a week over several years) we have to keep in mind that deeper "internal world" changes would not be possible and thus indeed not expected from severely mentally ill patients being exposed to the atmospheres espoused in this text. Not only would staff not be trained at this intensity, but also so many other factors impinge on the patients' internal world, from their experiences with other professionals, family members, and the lack of formality in a residential setting. Also, assuming that severely mentally ill patients live in the paranoid-schizoid position, only items listed in Table 1 could be used to quantify whether there is any movement from (as in the original scale) the items listed as "very characteristic" (rated 5) or "very uncharacteristic" (rated 1) of the patients' state of mind, before and after the treatment intervention. For example, the item "Destructive envy, spoiling, devaluation, and/or contempt" would be a common feature of psychotic transferences that occur in everyday relationships with severely mentally ill patients. Any lessening of this would be of benefit to both patients and staff and could conceivably emerge after a period of containment in a therapeutic atmosphere. Looking for a lessening of paranoid-schizoid functioning would be a realistic achievement when considering the severity of the state of mind being treated and the non-specific nature of the therapeutic atmosphere which is being offered to lessen the harshness and internal impoverishment of the patient. Some depressive position functioning may be achieved, but is not the aim of this particular treatment intervention. Lessening of paranoid-schizoid functioning would offer a small but significant easement in the patient's inner world.

## Quality of outcome measures scale

The quality of object relations scale described by Azim, Piper, Segal, Nixon, and Duncan (1991) has been extensively used in individual psychotherapy research (e.g., Piper, Joyce, McCollum, & Azim, 1993) to explore the effects of transference interpretations with patients exhibiting different qualities in how they related to themselves and others (object relations). Importantly, the scale is based on the theoretical work of Freud, Abraham, Klein, Fairbairn, Winnicott, and Bion. The scale to be reported here has been trialled and tested with both neurotic and psychotic patients. It consists of five organisational levels: mature, triangular, controlling, searching, and primitive. Criteria at each level are judged under four headings: behavioural manifestations, affect regulation, self-esteem regulation, and aetiological factors, for example, primitive level is characterised by:

- Inordinate dependence on an object, which is manifested in either clinging behaviour, or aloofness and distance, or both (one of seven behavioural manifestations).
- Preoccupation with destroying or being destroyed by the object, manifested by murderous rage and fear of annihilation (one of five criteria of affect regulation).
- Tendency towards idealisation and/or devaluation of self and of objects (one of the criteria of self-esteem regulation).
- Sexual or physical traumatisation (one of three criteria of antecedents).

In contrast and at the opposite end of the scale, the mature level is characterised by:

- Capacity to express love, tenderness, and concern for others of both sexes (one of three criteria of affect regulation).
- Self-esteem regulation based on equitable receiving from and giving to objects (only criteria of this characteristic).
- Good enough pre-Oedipal relationships and healthy resolution of the Oedipus complex, leading to identification with both parents and achieving "good enough" love object (only criteria of antecedents).

The measure is administered as a semi-structured interview by a clinician familiar with the theoretical framework. Here, the clinician would conduct a general discussion of the patient's personal history and current presentation. Azim, Piper, Segal, Nixon, and Duncan (1991) used a particular rating/scoring procedure that quantifies the overall grade of object relations at each particular level, arriving at a particular indicative score of nine (mature), seven (triangular), five (controlling), three (searching), and one (primitive). Any overall score below 4.5 signified a low quality of object relations.

This scale achieved good inter-rater reliability of 76 per cent and a Cohen's kappa coefficient of 0.52. The intraclass coefficient for the nine-point scale overall score was 0.5. While they indicated that the scale is not related to psychiatric disturbance as they correlated their scale with dimensions of the DSM III (Azim, Piper, Segal, Nixon, and Duncan, 1991), I would argue that object relations, particularly primitive, triangular, and controlling are very much related to psychiatric disturbance, and particularly with people suffering from severe mental illness. This of course would be consistent with the theoretical premise on which this text is based, that is, that poor quality object relations are embedded in, if not the cause of, severe mental illness.

With this in mind, I think (as in the previous measure) that aspects of this scale could be adopted to capture elements of the patient's internal world that may be affected by exposure to a therapeutic atmosphere. For example, adopting only the primitive level measure of object relations, before and after treatment, could capture some small but significant changes in the patient's state of mind which may ease his internal world (the aim of the therapeutic atmospheres proposed in this text).

### Micro-outcome findings

There is little or no empirical research into the effects of a Kleinian psychoanalytic interpretative approach or the state of mind of a severely mentally ill patient. My own postdoctoral work with Professor Peter Hobson (formerly of the Tavistock Clinic, London) compared and contrasted different conceptualisations of "transference" across British (Hobson & Kapur, 2005), American (Connolly et al., 1999), and Canadian (Piper, Joyce, McCollum, & Azim, 1993) research and found that different definitions were used, so questioning the generalisability of clinical and research findings in different professional/geographical settings. What I will report here is my micro-outcome research into the effects of Kleinian informed psychoanalytic interpretations.

### The effects of interpretations on individuals in psychotherapy with a paranoid-schizoid state of mind

This particular research is wholly based on the theoretical framework outlined in Chapter One of this book. I am indebted to Professor Hobson for giving me access to videotapes of individual psychotherapy assessments that he conducted at the Tavistock Clinic and for his support, supervision, and advice on this doctoral research. Without his generosity this research would not have been possible. Patients kindly gave permission for these tapes to be used and patient confidentiality was maintained at all times. The research to be reported constituted my doctoral dissertation (unpublished) with Birkbeck College, University of London (Kapur, 1998).

This process/outcome research is derived from Strachey's (1934) classic paper on mutative interpretations where he stated:

> By virtue of his power as auxiliary superego, the analyst gives permission for a certain small quantity of the patient's id-energy (in our instance, in the form of an aggressive impulse) to become conscious. Since the analyst is also, from the nature of things, the object of the patient's id-impulse, the quantity of these impulses which is now released into consciousness, will become consciously directed towards the analyst. This is the critical point if all goes well, the patient's ego will become aware of the contrast between the aggressive character of his feelings and the real nature of the analyst, who does not behave like the patient's "good" or "bad" archaic objects. The patient, that is to say, will become aware of a distinction between his archaic phantasy object and the real external object. The interpretation has now become a mutative one, since it has produced a breach in the neurotic vicious circle. For the patient, having become aware of the lack of aggressiveness in the real external object, will be able to diminish his own aggressiveness; the new object, which he introjects will be less aggressive and consequently, the aggressiveness of his superego will also be diminished. As a further corollary to these events and simultaneously with them, the patient will obtain access to the infantile material which is being re-experienced by him in relation to the analyst. (pp. 282–283)

The critical process variable here is the "interpretation" which in my research was defined as:

> ... a comment by the therapist to the individual which is directed towards bringing to the surface meanings of the communication that has occurred. An interpretation is a hypothesis by the therapist of the meaning of the utterance. This is scored on a 5 point scale on the following 2 dimensions, Transference (5) and Extra-Transference (1). (Kapur, 1998)

Subsequently, and based on the work of Sinason (1993) and Steiner (1993) the interpretation was scored on two other characteristics.

## Mapping

The interpretation is directed towards "mapping out" the state of mind of the patient, in relation to the patient and therapist dyad. If the therapist is describing two different states of mind then this is scored as five and if only one whole state of mind, then this is scored as one.

This is specifically aimed at capturing Bion's (1952) concept of "psychotic" and "non-psychotic" personalities, so aptly described in Sinason's (1993) paper. The idea is to convey an understanding with a mapping interpretation that whatever the grip of the psychotic personality, there is a non-psychotic personality (sane self) that desperately wants help or to be rescued (Rosenfeld, 1987) but is trapped by the influence of the psychotic personality. An example would be:

> "I think there is a part of you that would like to come to the sessions and finds it helpful, though there is another part that feels furious that you need to depend on someone for help."

A non-mapping interpretation would be:

> "I think you just want to destroy our relationship, completely spoil anything good."

## Centredness

The other characteristic of the interpretative process variable that was measured was "centredness". This is specifically based on the work of John Steiner (1993). His key theoretical idea is of an emotional retreat that the patient inhabits to deal with external emotional life. He writes:

> A psychic retreat provides the patient with an area of relative peace and protection from strain when meaningful contact with the analyst is experienced as threatening. It is not difficult to understand the need for transient withdrawal of this kind but serious technical problems arise in patients who turn to a psychic retreat, habitually, excessively and indiscriminately. In some analyses, particularly with borderline and psychotic patients, a more or less permanent residence in the retreat may be taken up and it is then that obstacles to development and growth arise. (p. 1)

He goes on to describe how such patients relate to the analyst in a distant, aloof, superior, and often condescending way. Their internal world contains a "pathological organisation" that is opposed to any real contact and he suggests a particular interpretative style is required to let the patient know he has been "understood" in respect of how persecutory and threatening a patient may experience an ordinary interpretation. He writes:

> Experience suggests that such (therapeutic) containment is weakened if the analyst perseveres in interpreting or explaining to the patient what he is thinking, feeling or doing. The patient experiences such interpretations as a lack of containment and feels the analyst is pushing the projected elements back into him. (p. 132)

Technically, he suggests the analyst speaks to the patient in a way that "understands" how he was experienced, such as:

> "You experience me as ..."
>     "You are afraid that I ..."
>     "You heard me saying you were bad ..."

These "analyst centred" interpretations were described as "centredness" interpretations in this research and scored a five with, scored as one, "ordinary patient centred" interpretations such as:

> "I think you are worried about what happens here."
>     "It seems you feel distant and detached here."

The effects of these interpretative styles were captured by operationalising and measuring two key concepts: paranoid-schizoid functioning and attacks on linking. These constitute the micro-outcome or dependent variables in this research. After revisiting the Kleinian and post-Kleinian framework, the following triangle of variables was adopted to capture the impact of an interpretation (Figure 3).

## Linking

> The main conclusion of the paper relates to that state of mind in which the patient's psyche contains an internal object which is

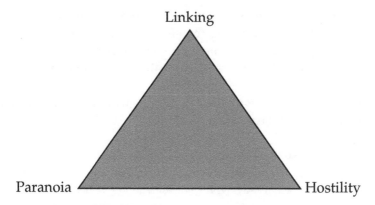

Figure 3. Measuring the effect of an interpreation.

opposed to, and destructive of, all links whatsoever from the most
primitive to the most sophisticated forms of verbal communication
and the arts. (Bion, 1967, p. 108)

In this paper on "Attacks on Linking", Bion focuses on how the healthy
links that occur between analyst and patient, as well as within the
patient, are exposed by the very disturbed "psychotic" part of the
patient's personality. He writes:

I have had occasions in talking to the psychotic part of the personality, to speak of the destructive attacks which the patient makes on
anything which is felt to have the functioning of linking one object
to another. (p. 93)

I think what Bion is trying to capture is the depth of human contact characteristic of the depressive position, which in a well-known
phrase appears as "tenderness I cannot bear". It is this linking or
coupling that I am trying to capture with the patient's response to
an interpretation. Good linkage should develop with a "good mutative interpretation", which is characterised by a full understanding of
the patient's state of mind. In the research protocol this is defined as
follows:

A ring of a chain, anything connecting, to connect, to be or become
connected. (Chambers Dictionary, 1975)

Linking refers to the degree of mutual relatedness between therapist and patient. Both are working together as a couple in an emotional and productive way which may be characterised by positive and negative feelings. There is a reciprocal process between therapist and patient.

If a patient is linking with the therapist, he would respond in the following way to an interpretation:

> "When you spoke to me about how I can treat you badly and how this is linked to my suspiciousness of you, that felt right. I understand what you are saying. It's not something I've been aware of. This has really brought it to my awareness, something I know more about." (Scored as high linking, five.)

A "low linking" and potentially an "attack on linking" would be:

> "That's not true; you're always getting at me. You talk nonsense when I'm here. What's the point, I don't really think you give a damn about me." (Scored as low linking, one.)

All scores are post-interpretation.

### Paranoia

> Psychopathology of everyday life abounds in examples of paranoid delusions. We are all apt to feel at times, that it always rains when we have planned to spend a day out of doors, that the bus going in the opposite direction to ours, always comes first, that some unfortunate experience we have had was directly due to somebody's ill will or at least to fate. Usually, however, this type of paranoid delusion is easily corrected … . Following this line of thought we come to discern a rising scale of severity in delusional attitudes. There is a momentary reaction—"Damn that fool." Ascending the scale, there is the mood which may persist for some hours—"I knew everything would go wrong with me today and it has!" Neither of these leads, as yet, to harmful consequences, both are entirely compatible with sound mental health. Next in severity might be a paranoid state lasting for days or weeks, or more. Finally, there is the psychosis in which the person's life is totally determined by

his belief in a persecution, the delusion having become permanent, and the focus of a rigid system. (Heimann, 1956, p. 240)

This quote from Paula Heimann describes the paranoid characteristics of the personality of the patient which is being measured in this research, as one of the three dependent variables. A post-Kleinian analyst, Grotstein (1979) elaborates on this negative state of mind:

> This paranoia is the underlying element of *all* psychopathology and the attainment of the depressive position is its cure. This is another way of stating that the essential construction of all psychopathology is based on schizoid splits of internal objects which are believed to control the self (and also, in their degraded form, are controlled by the self). The cosmos of these internal objects is essentially controlling and persecutory. From this standpoint, all psychopathological conditions vary essentially in how they experience their internal persecutors. (p. 433)

In the rating scale, the effects of an interpretation were measured by the difference or "before and after interpretation" score on paranoia (and the following variable of aggression). The definition is as follows:

> "Paranoia is used to describe a state of mind within the patient characterised by suspicion and fear. The patient is intensely distrustful and is convinced that others are intent on harming him/her. There is a great fear of persecution. There is no confidence in the idea that the patient is being helped."

Examples are as follows:
  High paranoia (scored as five):

> "You're not interested in me; all you want to do is criticise me and tell me off. Why should I listen to you; you're only sent to get me. Everyone hates me, everyone is my enemy."

Low paranoia (scored as one) or trustfulness would be:

> "I do trust you now. I feel you are here to help me, not to persecute me."

## Aggression

Kleinian theory, as described in Chapter One, places critical importance on the role of aggression/hostility in the person's relation to himself and others. Melanie Klein, in taking further Freud's original theories of "identifying with the aggressor", sought to explore the early relationship between mother and infant. She remarks on the common phantasies held by children of being eaten by a wolf, or fire-spewing dragons, as examples of how early aggressive impulses can remain unmodified to create terrors in the child. In her paper, "The Early Development of Conscience in the Child" (1933), she writes:

> In penetrating to the deepest layers of the child's mind and discovering those terrors of being attacked in all sorts of ways, we also lay bare a corresponding amount of repressed impulses of aggression and can observe their causal connection, which exists between the child's fears and its aggressive tendencies ... the foundation stone for the development of the superego, whose excessive violence in this early stage would thus be accounted for by the fact that it is an off-shoot of very intense destructive instincts and contains, along with a certain proportion of libidinal impulses, very large quantities of aggressive ones. (pp. 248–250)

It is through the introjection/experience of a benevolent, thoughtful, and understanding interpretation that this hostility may ease. She writes:

> Then perhaps (after successful psychoanalytic therapy), that hostile attitude, springing from fear and suspicion, which is latent more or less strongly in each human being and which intensifies a hundred-fold in him every impulse of destruction, will give way to kindlier and more trustful feelings towards his fellow man and people may inhabit the world together in greater peace and good-will than they do now. (p. 257)

In this research the following definition is used:

> "Aggression—A first act of hostility, injury, offensive as opposed to defensive, disorderly, hostile or self-assertive." (Chambers Dictionary, 1975)

The patient *overtly* slows aggressive feelings. This refers to hostility, negativity from the patient which may be directed towards the therapist. The patient used words to attribute negative emotions to himself and others which may be towards the extreme aggression of hatred.

High aggression (scored as five) would be:

> "I hate your guts when you talk about me depending on you, why do you have to rub it in? Sometimes I feel like hitting you, knocking that smugness off your face."

Non-aggression (scored as one) would be:

> "I think the sessions are helpful. I look forward to them now. I can speak to you much better and we can try and sort things out that I will talk about."

As noted earlier, it is the different score before and after the interpretation that is used as the raw data.

This triangle of dependent variables was chosen to reflect the validity of everyday clinical interactions in the practice of interpretative, psychoanalytic psychotherapy, with "disturbed and difficult" states of mind. I think it has great usefulness empirically and clinically in assessing both the impact of interpretations and the patient's state of mind. Patients who are suspicious and hostile will not link fully with the psychotherapist offering this particular style of psychoanalytic work, where good, full, and benevolent interpretations are offered in the spirit of understanding the patient and so easing his distressed state of mind. However, if the interpretation is partially or fully introjected, the hostility and paranoia may lessen, so allowing fuller "links" to take place where there is a depth and quality to the human relations between the analyst and patient established in therapeutic work. Alternatively, as highlighted in the text "Attacks on Linking", it may be that the interpretative activity may elicit a negative response.

## Research findings

Table 6 presents the final inter-rater reliabilities for the three independent and three dependent variables.

Table 5. Inter-rater reliabilities for variables.[1]

| Variable | Correlation coefficient[2] |
| --- | --- |
| Transference | 0.7 |
| Mapping | 0.64 |
| Centredness | 0.61 |
| Paranoia | 0.6 |
| Aggression | 0.52 |
| Linking | 0.51 |

[1] In earlier versions of the coding manual, envy, contempt, guilt, and concern were operationalised, but achieved low levels of inter-rater reliability, 0.13, 0.21, 0.003, and 0.16 respectively and thus were dropped.

[2] Intra-class coefficients (Shrout & Fleiss, 1979) were calculated.

Two judges who had a knowledge of this theoretical framework were asked to rate therapist and patient episodes of speech. Data for the operationalisation and measurement of these variables were taken from process recordings of my own psychotherapy sessions. The precursor to this conceptualisation was data gathered from group psychotherapy sessions with severely mentally ill patients.

Two of the six variables achieved moderate agreement between two raters (aggression and linking), with the other four variables achieving substantial agreement. In other words, it was possible for two judges to agree on what constituted these variables when judging psychotherapy transcripts. This is significant for two reasons. First and what is important, it confirms that it is possible to operationalise and measure concepts within this particular Kleinian theoretical framework. Second, these findings confirm that it is possible to reliably explore the immediate effects of interpretations on the state of mind of the patient.

Table 6 presents correlation coefficients for eight assessments patients (video tape sessions carried out by Professor Hobson) and three treatment patients in ongoing psychotherapy.

The main findings for these results are:

• There is no empirical evidence to confirm the immediate effects of a mutative interpretation.
• It may be that any theoretically predicted effect can occur later in the session, or in treatment as a delayed effect.

Table 6.  Correlation coefficients for all patients.

|  | Linking | Paranoia | Aggression |
|---|---|---|---|
| Transference | 0.002 (n = 874) | 0.02 (n = 895) | −0.06 (n = 895) |
| Mapping | 0.01 (n = 203) | −0.2* (n = 202) | −0.14* (n = 202) |
| Centredness | 0.11 (n = 198) | −0.02 (n = 197) | −0.03 (n = 197) |

*P < 0.05

- Theoretically and dogmatically sticking to a psychotherapeutic technique may not be justified as "wanted" effects may simply not exist.
- The "paranoia, aggression, linking" triangle of clinical micro-outcomes may be a helpful conceptual and empirical tool to gauge the effects of interpretative activity.

While the pooled data for the eleven patients (Table 6) did reveal some slight but significant correlations for mapping with paranoia and aggression, that is, mapped out interpretations may be associated with less paranoia and hostility from the patient as they may feel more "understood" (and vice versa), this is not a clear empirical finding as only two correlations emerged from the whole data suggesting this may be due to chance. However, the finding would be worthy of further research and if confirmed would support the theoretical ideas behind this interpretative style (Sinason, 1993).

In conclusion, the following can be determined from this research:

> It is possible to reliably operationalise and measure variables derived from a Kleinian theoretical framework. There is no empirical evidence to suggest that working in the transference is more effective than working outside the transference. A clinically useful conceptual triangle of micro-outcome measures of linking, aggression, and paranoia may be helpful to judge the impact of interpretative activity. There is a possibility, albeit small and requiring much more research, that "mapping out" the oppositional and co-operative states of mind of the patient may help the patient feel more understood and thus lessen more feelings of hostility and suspiciousness. It may also be that as the patient feels less hostile and suspicious, the therapist maps out his state of mind.

# CHAPTER SEVEN

# Consultancy and external expertise

A s those of us who have been on the couch know, being on the receiving end of another person's external analysis of your mind is a delicate process. Furthermore, if you and I or the patient decide to invite the external agent into your mind (internal world), a delicate and complex process unfolds where every nuance of the transference/countertransference relationship has to be analysed to facilitate psychic change (Joseph, 1975) from the paranoid-schizoid to the depressive position (assuming that the analyst or therapist is working within the theoretical framework described in Chapter One of this text). This analytic process occurs through specialist training and the help of supervisors and peers. I will give you a recollection of my own transference/countertransference reaction when I was on an academic visit to approve and inspect a psychology/clinical psychology university department.

"I arrived at the university having been depleted in my own work place by conflict between junior staff and board members, where I felt my word meant nothing. The sniping and undermining of my authority left me feeling pretty bad ... and then I had this scheduled visit as a QAA (Quarterly Assurance Agency) inspector and was greeted as if I was someone of great importance. The best hotel and food were provided and every word I uttered was held on to, from vice-chancellor to lecturer. I felt valued!"

Inviting an external consultant into your organisation is fraught with difficulty, particularly if no preparatory work takes place to ensure precise roles and responsibilities, defining what the external consultant is invited to do and not do. Will he act on the countertransference reaction of feeling important and project unwanted psychotic parts into the organisation (paranoid-schizoid functioning) or will he act in a humble and modest way in recognising the good parts of the organisation and offer some "food for thought" on things that can be improved upon and not interfere with management responsibilities (depressive position). In Table 7, I highlight definitions of good and bad authority, superimposed upon Hobson, Patrick, and Valentine's (1998) operational definitions of paranoid-schizoid and depressive position functioning. These aspects refer equally to internal and external authority and I will explore some of these in detail with examples (critical incidents 1–6). I will conclude the chapter by using three ideas, two from the clinical psychoanalytic literature and the other, the "state of mind" concept cited in the Introduction. Both highlight important processes to achieve depressive position functioning.

## Psychotic and non-psychotic contributions

As in the premise behind Bion's (1961) "work group", everyone in a group or organisation has a contribution to make. As in conducting a group, it is important to elicit and value the contribution of others and then decide on their value and worth. What I have found, using Bion's terminology, is that it is crucial to differentiate between psychotic (destructive) versus non-psychotic (creative) contributions. I have often witnessed external consultants failing miserably to differentiate between staff members who wish to undermine the authority of the agency and myself as CEO, and collude destructively against management, and sincerely genuine contributions from others. An exchange highlights this:

## Critical incident 1

"This middle manager was astute and cunning in playing the helpless victim while all the time scooping out the goodness of the agency. He

Table 7. Definitions of good and bad authority.

| Good authority | Bad authority |
|---|---|
| • Respecting the contribution of everyone: "What you say matters". | • "Your views mean nothing." |
| • Concern for subordinates. | • Staff are numbers, what you say doesn't matter. |
| • Willingness to deal with the complexity of manager/worker relationships. | • Idealisation/devaluation of staff. |
| • Willingness to acknowledge when you are wrong. | • Controlling and paranoid. |
| • Straight/trustworthy. | • Envious attacks on the achievements of others. |
| • Recognising the "ordinary and sane" needs of staff. | • Narcissistic. |
| • Not abusing others' dependency of your being in authority. | • Omnipotent and omniscience. |
| • Benevolent authority. | • Persecution as the main style of management. |
| • Emotionally and intellectually integrated. | • Unable to "hold uncertainty" until a solution emerges. |
| • Capacity to "let things go" and reflect. | • Constant anxiety that "things will break down/go wrong". |
| • Accepting the aloneness of the role. | • Explosive rage when things aren't done or instructions followed. |
| • Feeling "job well done" as a source of narcissistic nourishment. | • Competitive. |

was a master of disguise and revelled in treating the external consultant as someone who could be easily fooled. This contribution was subversive, seductive, but completely missed by the external consultant."

External consultants, many of whom in the psychoanalytic world work in private practice (completely outside and without management experience of organisations), project onto organisational life the stereotypical view of the "bad boss", as occurred in this example. Society will propagate this view, thus leaving a manager vulnerable to overcompensating for a projection that does not belong to him. I have also found when inviting externals from the world of psychoanalysis and psychotherapy, there can be an envious attack on management as they have never held, and are unlikely to hold such a role. So for the external consultant to offer an experience of good authority, he must act within his own limitations, differentiate between destructive and creative contributions, and be aware of envy in himself and others that can undermine the work of the organisation.

Conversely, an experience of "bad authority" is where the genuine and creative contributions of others are devalued, which invariably is an envious attack. A personal example illustrates this:

### Critical incident 2

"As CEO of Threshold I thought my contribution to my own agency was helpful. This was not the view of an external consultant, whom I invited in from a 'reputable' company, with 'expertise' in this field. Staff, unbeknown to me, had painted me as a dictator and bully without the consultant being aware of the dysfunctional and undermining performance of these staff. They portrayed themselves as 'victims', which was believed. More seriously, my executive authority as company director with legal responsibility for the agency was completely undermined."

Any external (consultant) or internal (manager) authority must carefully weigh up and think through (alpha process) the contributions of all staff and then proceed carefully as to their own input to the agency. Envy must be analysed by the external consultant to ensure he is not acting out his own limitations and failings. Similarly, when highlighting areas of potential difficulty (which may or may not be accurate) he has to be reasonably confident that he is not acting out the destructive feelings of staff. Kane (2012) draws attention to this process and how it presents itself under the guise of manic superiority and belittlement, all the time hiding personal and professional failures that are well covered by the ferocity and accuracy of an envious attack to the Achilles heel of the victim. She writes:

> Those who are subject to envious feelings cannot allow themselves to know that they are envious. Envy is so deeply shameful that exposure is profoundly humiliating and the envious person will go to any lengths to deny having these feelings, indeed, the denial is often so profound that those envious feelings are not allowed to emerge into conscious thinking of the envious person. (p. 207)

In organisational life, this has huge consequences for the services delivered, because if the manager is the envied person, then account-ability and standards of performance will be undermined and compromised.

## Concern

As stated above, I have found that external consultants, particularly when commenting on organisational issues, often overidentify with junior staff as "oppressed human beings". They then neglect and ignore the pressures on the CEO and senior managers, who are ordinary human beings under greater pressure to ensure the organisation func-tions properly. Massive splitting occurs where staff are seen as victims of bad authority. I think these pressures are particularly acute in the voluntary sector where it operates as an independent company that will succeed or fail on the executive decisions of senior managers (Tyler, 2006). I will describe a "perfect storm" where an external consultant completely failed to recognise the pressures on me when the organisa-tion faced a major crisis.

## Critical incident 3

"Senior staff were tasked with setting up a new project. Despite assur-ances to the contrary, they totally failed to consult with commissioners and key stakeholders. Referrals failed to materialise and so the project itself failed miserably. The senior staff responsible for the agency por-trayed themselves as victims to the consultant, who was employed in an advisory capacity to the agency. The consultant had no financial or legal insight into the operations of an independent company. He showed no concern nor had he the capacity to reflect on the enormity of the effect this had on senior managers left to pick up the pieces. The agency was on the brink of insolvency, i.e. not able to pay its bills."

Threshold did not sink; it rejuvenated itself with alternative income streams to its current strong financial position today. However, in this "perfect storm" the external consultant failed to treat the CEO (myself) as an ordinary human being, inheriting a mess created by inefficiency and poor planning (no formal contracts had been established and thus funding was "on a wing and a prayer"). It is imperative that exter-nal consultants adopt the depressive position from "top to bottom", otherwise they will become unwitting partners with basic assumption pairing and/or fight/flight, which will undermine the leadership of the organisation. This also potentially re-enacts early familial conflicts against "bad parents" from staff acting as anti-authority rebellious children.

Similarly, for internal authority processes, there has to be a reciprocity between senior, middle, and junior staff of concern for others with shared goals, rather than upward and outward "part-object" dehumanisation of people as numbers. This is a complex task as staff at all levels have to consistently remember:

- Whatever the hierarchical level of the person, each is an ordinary human being with strengths and weaknesses.
- Saying "I don't know", "I need your help", and taking responsibility when things go wrong is a strength, not a weakness.
- Every individual will have good days and bad days affected by personal and professional pressures.
- Criticism or belittlement will always have a negative effect; better to circumvent any failings by exploring other solutions.
- Projecting inadequacies onto others only leads to a vicious cycle of disillusionment.

The onus is, of course, on management to maintain the depressive position. However, an important part of this, like working with a psychiatric patient, is being a "brick mother" and showing firm boundaries to manage paranoid-schizoid functioning from staff that is not corrected with management instruction, direction, or insight. While a negative organisational reaction may ensue, the ultimate personal responsibility (legally and morally) does rest with the most senior manager to ensure that safe and effective care is being delivered to patients.

## Complexity vs. naïve simplicity

Every organisation has its own individuality and personality and must be treated as such, whether it is in the voluntary, statutory, or private sector. Often assumptions are made about all three service providers with little thought given to the critical functions of each service which affect patient delivery. In my experience of all these sectors, the main differences which impact greatly on service delivery are financial and who the customer/key stakeholders are (Table 8 highlights these different complexities). Within the health and social care services of the NHS there is an assumption that funding is recurrent and generally exists as a permanent source of income. While cutbacks in the NHS have been more frequent recently, the overall services do not operate as a business or limited company. This contrasts greatly with the voluntary and private sectors. The former operates on a "not for profit" framework but is mainly controlled by contracts it has to fulfil with its purchasers/commissioners. In Threshold's case, this is mainly through the N. Ireland Housing Executive's Supporting People scheme along with some "care top-ups" from the local health trusts. Failure to meet occupancy and service delivery targets directly leads to a loss of income and thus service. (In its twenty-five year history, Threshold has had to close down three residential projects.) In contrast in the private sector, where most psychoanalytic psychotherapy is based, the means of the patient decides whether a service can be delivered. Private wealth also determines the training opportunities for professionals specialising in this area.

The key aspect of this analysis is that any external consultant must take into account the nature of the service he is consulting to, otherwise incorrect assumptions may be made that could seriously impact upon service delivery. An example is as follows:

## Critical incident 4

"A private psychotherapist who was involved with the organisation (Threshold) in a training capacity and with no real grasp of how public

Table 8. Complexity of organisational processes.

| Sector | Financial | Key customers/stakeholders |
|--------|-----------|----------------------------|
| Statutory (NHS) | Does not operate as a limited company. Government funded. | Public sector accountability to patients. |
| Voluntary | Operates as a limited company and has to pursue and secure contracts for payment. | Public and statutory commissioners (health, housing, and social care). |
| Private | Wholly operates as an individual business with little or no commitment to public service. Only accountable to itself. | Fee paying patients—no contracts or research. |

money must be used for 'public good', approached the organisation asking to establish an accreditation for a psychotherapy training to be used wholly for the needs of private patients. No cognisance was given to the contractual obligations of the agency to adhere to the requirements of our public sector commissioners. He had no understanding of Threshold's accountability or awareness that the agency's funding could, potentially, have been put at risk by complying with such a request."

It is essential for the external consultant to fully grasp the complexity of any organisational setting. Failure to do so will lead to the organisation making mistakes which will adversely affect services and in some cases cause their reduction or cancellation. Assumptions cannot be made that every organisation operates with the same financial or stakeholder specification.

## Ordinary hard work vs. idealised narcissistic noise

For any analytic thinker, operating within the context of the theoretical framework outlined in Chapter One, effective alpha processing is characterised by intensely concentrating on "projected particles" from the patient and giving something back that can be introjected to create thought and emotional movement at some depth. Unfortunately, this rarely occurs in normal organisational life, and external and internal authority figures are prone to get caught up in action-driven solutions to complex issues, without the ordinary hard work of "thinking things through" and recognising the complexities of processes that affect outcome. A typical meeting that I have attended in the public sector is as follows:

## Critical incident 5

"The chairman arrived late as did most of the remaining professionals attending the meeting. The agenda was scheduled for three hours, with no breaks. Bundles of papers were distributed that could not possibly be read during the meeting. Agenda items were hijacked by individuals telling stories of their own 'pet issue'. Chaos ensued and the agenda was not completed. People left early. During the meeting individuals were using their iPhones to email and communicate with people inside and outside the meeting. There was no order."

Good authority (external and internal) should be characterised by the features of a good analytic frame.

- Starting with each issue in an orderly and thoughtful way.
- Avoiding overexcitement and narcissistic responses to issues.
- Listening carefully and recognising the contributions of everyone and, as stated above, differentiating between destructive (psychotic) and creative/helpful (non-psychotic) contributions.
- Recognising the breadth and complexity of issues and not overloading the space to talk and think about things.

The quality of discourse, particularly as delivered by those in authority, will dictate the outcome of organisational processes. Those acting as external consultants will often be under pressure to deliver big results quickly rather than quietly leave an organisation or team with one or two main issues to think about in order to introduce ordinary, incremental change to processes that affect outcome. An example of a "thought through" issue is as follows:

## Critical incident 6

"Staff morale was low as some staff had left and found employment elsewhere as well as some others who were on sick leave. There was a depressed, victim atmosphere in the room among several other managers. As the chair of the group, I was tempted to inject some 'positive thinking' into the meeting. However, I let the 'issue quietly sit' with a recognition that this is always a difficult reality to accept in operating any service. Patients would not get a good service and we had a responsibility to improve things. We were failing our patients. Then a manager, unbeknown to me, who had a full staff team, offered her own time and that of another member to help. The depressed mood was released and there was an idea that we could help each other out at difficult moments rather than inject an overexcited and temporary 'Elastoplast' response to an issue."

I think those given the role of chair or other authoritative role (internally or externally) in an organisation must avoid being a noisy and narcissistic problem solver to complex difficulties that exist in everyday work life. Where possible, they have to allow for and facilitate creative thinking and coupling that leads to new ideas and organisational growth. Ordinary thinking, in the depressive position, will often provide solutions within an organisation, particularly in an atmosphere devoid of noise and narcissism that can only lead to the likelihood of poor outcomes.

### Dependency and vulnerability

Whether it is in the analytic, organisational, or personal setting, depending on someone else always involves a degree of vulnerability from the one depending on an other with perceived greater or real resources. Much depends on the personal history of staff as to whether they can rely on others. As described in Chapter One, self-sufficiency is the state of mind of the narcissistic who "needs nobody but uses everyone" for his own need to be recognised and valued. Mutual and reciprocal dependency in a spirit of the depressive position is a rare commodity in organisational life. However, if this can be facilitated and nurtured it can lead to huge organisational gains.

When inviting an external consultant into your organisation, the issue of vulnerability is huge, particularly if the consultant does not take into account, understand, and seriously accept the complexity of the services he is consulting to. Thirdness or a three-dimensional view will ensure that the overall picture is being considered in an iterative fashion, to ensure there is a live, fluid, and accurate understanding at any particular moment. By thirdness/three-dimensional I mean keeping in mind that in any dialogue there will always be "other" factors influencing decisions. This is particularly the case in the organisational life of statutory, private, and voluntary sectors, where the management of staff has to occur within the context of employment law (see Chapter Nine) which is always the inevitable but powerful presence in the room. I will return to the clinical literature to highlight the emergence of thirdness in each of us, as described by Britton (1989) who has written extensively on this. He writes:

> The primal family triangle provides the child with two links connecting him separately with each parent and confronts him with the link between them which excludes him. Initially this parental link is conceived in primitive part-object terms and in modes of his own oral, anal and genital desires, and in terms of his hatred

expressed in oral, anal and genital terms. If the link between the parents perceived in love and hate can be tolerated in the child's mind, it provides him with a prototype for an object relationship of a third kind in which he is a witness and not a participant. A third position then comes into existence from which object relationships can be observed. Given this, we can also envisage *being* observed. This provides us with a capacity for seeing ourselves in interaction with others and for entertaining another point of view whilst retaining our own, for reflecting on ourselves whilst being ourselves. (p. 87)

If an organisation depends on an external consultant, a junior member of staff depends on a senior member of staff, or a CEO depends on his/her chairperson, then it is imperative that in a discussion of every issue, another issue can be kept in mind. As an example, in discussing how patients are being treated, we have to keep in mind the limited resources available when working in a voluntary agency. When consulting on poor staff performance between a manager and staff member, we have to keep in mind employment law. When advising a senior manager on how to manage a difficult staff member, we need to keep in mind that "difficult and bad parts" can belong to both parties. Objectivity is maximised by having the capacity to reflect in this "third way" on the issues. If this third way can be maintained then there is a much greater chance of depressive position functioning where many complex issues can be thought about that influence the overall state of mind of an organisation.

## Overvalued ideas, selected facts, and missing data

It is impossible for any external or internal authority figure to have all the relevant information to hand. In research terminology, there will always be "missing data". However, in psychoanalytic thinking it is about making the best judgement of what is a selected fact or interpretation of reality without it becoming an overvalued idea (I only want to believe in something because it's my favourite theory).

It was Bion (1962) who coined the phrase "selected fact". He writes:

If a new result is to have any value, it must unite elements long since known, but till then, scattered and seemingly foreign to each other and then suddenly introduce order where the appearance of disorder reigned. Then it enables us to see at a glance each of these elements in the place it occupies in the whole. Not only is the new fact vulnerable on its own account, but it alone gives a value to the old facts it unites ... . The only facts worthy of our attention are those which introduce order into this complexity and so make it accessible to us. (p. 72)

In organisations, managers have to tolerate lots of uncertainty (negative capability) to allow the multiplicity of elements to form into a fact that is as near the truth (no matter how painful and difficult) as possible. An example of managing a particular member of staff highlights this:

## Critical incident 7

"I had invested heavily, with good faith and goodwill, in a new member of staff who had presented at interview with an 'all bells and whistles' presentation. Somewhere I knew that manic presentations can hide inadequacy and dishonesty. However, I ignored those 'elements' and went along with the view of the other panel members and appointed the candidate thinking to myself it was not the time to be risk averse. So I continued on with my professional faith and the organisation's financial investment. Then slowly other unwanted elements began to emerge, like exaggerated expense claims and inappropriate trips to conferences and meetings. When all these elements were put together, it emerged that this person was using the organisation's resources to gain further training and set up his own business."

Holding unwelcome facts to arrive at an "unthinkable thought", which leads to the emergence of a selected fact that can be tested in reality to decide whether it is a painful truth, is part and parcel of the depressive position functioning. It can lead to more effective decisions but requires the manager or external consultant to consider all information and withhold the wish to "prove a theory" or "overvalue an idea" (Britton & Steiner, 1994). In other words, minimising the possibility of arriving at conclusions that are based only on scant, narrow, and one-dimensional elements or pieces of information.

## State of mind

The central tenet of this theoretical framework is that the person in authority, whether it is a manager or external consultant, has to withstand the pressures of facing and receiving the breadth, depth, and destructiveness of paranoid-schizoid functioning and respond with a depressive position state of mind. In clinical work this is a demanding role, but in organisational work it is ever more pressurised as judgements, and thus decisions, have to be made under the legal, financial, and ultimately service delivery demands (particularly in the voluntary sector). The person with ultimate authority, the CEO, has to manage multiple and complex internal and external forces to deliver the best outcomes for those in his care. For this to be done properly, it requires (as in clinical work) much oscillation between paranoid-schizoid and depressive position functioning to ultimately arrive at a state of mind that reaches the most thoughtful and considered judgement. In my experience this is rare in organisational life.

Whether it is an external consultant or a manager, the following characteristics of their countertransference reaction have to be considered:

- Allow yourself to be affected by the state of mind of the organisation.
- In processing the effect of the organisation, allow yourself to oscillate between negative and positive views before settling on what you believe to be the "truth" of the predominant style of relating (paranoid-schizoid or depressive).
- Carefully decide on a small but significant intervention which can help people think about how they relate to themselves and others.

As in clinical work, the intervention is best delivered with the absence of wanting individuals to change (as in Bion's (1962) dictum of "no memory, no desire"), but rather in maximising the possibility that people will "stop and think" about the effect (often negative) that they are having on others.

## Critical incident 8

"A member of staff had jeopardised the care of patients through the mishandling of resources. The reputation of the agency was at risk as purchasers/commissioners were obviously concerned as to whether the organisation had proper controls in place. Colleagues wanted to 'run away' from the issue or retaliate and get rid of the member of staff. An external consultant suggested that perhaps this staff member had become the unwitting vehicle for acting out hidden wishes to rob the agency of its goodness, and while the issue had to be managed firmly (through the agency's 'Terms & Conditions of Employment') the incident represented what is always an issue in any organisation: to take only (rob), to give overenthusiastically (overidentify with the patient), or engage in a balanced reciprocity of 'give and take' (our livelihood is looking after patients, so let's work in the best way possible)."

In this incident the external consultant did his job by carefully considering the issues, naming the two extremes (robbing and overidentification), and then arriving at the preferred depressive position style of relating, where there is a two-way, ordinary, and reciprocal approach between staff and patients. If this is achieved, then there is a much better chance that the patient will be treated with concern, rather than as an object to earn a livelihood from or to be so overidentified with that the patient is meeting the needs of the staff member in an overdependent and dysfunctional way.

Essentially, for authority figures to be effective, they have to contain intense paranoid-schizoid functioning from the organisation (envy, projection, projective identification, and negative/psychotic transferences), identify healthy depressive position functioning, where real rather than false work is occurring, and work hard to think through their own emotional containment to ensure they respond from the depressive position with a combination of firmness and understanding, contingent on each particular circumstance. It is these projective/introjective moments that will dictate the quality of the working atmosphere which will have a direct bearing on the therapeutic atmosphere that we provide for our patients.

# CHAPTER EIGHT

# Management and leadership issues*

## Introduction

G roup analysts such as Blackwell (1998), Nitsun (1988, 1996), and Wilke (1998), along with psychoanalysts such as Kernberg (1980, 2003) and Obholzer and Roberts (2002) have attempted to bring psychoanalytic ideas to understanding organisations. However, nearly all mainstream management training relies on the implicit assumption that human beings will relate in a sane, reasonable, and rational way. In management and financial terminology this "critical assumption" is clearly false. Again, using traditional management theory of strategic planning, the internal world of human beings is rarely clearly aligned to the external world of the organisation. In other words what people feel and think may not be aligned with organisational objectives. Internal worlds will not simply align themselves to the aims and objectives of the organisation as written out in the traditional business plan. The neat and tidy jargon of management training fails to take account of the

---

* This chapter is a version of my 2009 paper entitled "Managing Primitive Emotions in Organisations" with a wholly revised discussion.

reality of human relations that need to be analysed carefully to create a healthy working environment.

I write this paper both as a chief executive and director, clinical psychologist, and psychoanalytic psychotherapist running an organisation within N. Ireland. Elsewhere I have written on how psychoanalytic ideas, particularly those of Melanie Klein can be applied to societal functioning (Kapur, 2001; Kapur & Campbell, 2004), and its application to the psychic life of organisations is no less relevant. The reality in running any organisation, no matter how small or large, is that the achievement of a work group (Bion, 1961), where staff are working fully towards fulfilling the main tasks of the organisation and where there is a capacity for concern for colleagues (Klein, 1946), is rare.

To create an atmosphere where there exists a minimum of splitting, projection, devaluation, and idealisation, and where human concern for others can flourish, is a complex and difficult task for a leader of any organisation to achieve (Shapiro, 2001). This is even more so in a society like N. Ireland, where there are tremendous regressive paranoid-schizoid pressures, so increasing the possibility that an autocratic style of management is idealised (Kapur & Campbell, 2004). For a psychologist, there is often the attraction towards assuming that neat conceptual frameworks can resolve deeper conflicts. For example, human resource practice would advocate valuing and supporting staff with the idea that it always produces a better outcome. However, if you have members of staff who suffer from borderline and narcissistic disorders, the human and financial resources of the organisation can be drained rapidly, so leaving an organisation weak and liable to collapse.

In this chapter I will review the main contributions to applying psychoanalytic ideas to organisations, highlight key "love and hate" dynamics within organisational life using psychoanalytic theory to describe the power of these processes, and then analyse organisational traumas I have experienced and my analysis and resolution of these. I will specifically focus on the analysis of psychotic processes as they appear in all organisations (Schwartz, 1990; Stapley, 1996). While the organisational scenarios I describe are from my experiences in mental health organisations where these can actively stir up the damaged and mad side of staff (Campling, 2004) the paper may have universal applications for other organisational situations.

## Psychoanalysis and organisations

The group analytic approach to understanding organisations has
relied mainly on the application of Foulkes's model of group analysis. Nitsun (1996) details the intervention used to reflect back to
the group what is happening as a modification of the traditional
group analytic technique of mirroring, whereby in organisations
the conductor identifies pathological resonances and distortions
that have a destructive effect so that roles and tasks can constructively be changed to ensure that feedback is used to improve the
organisational milieu.

The aim of this intervention is to analyse organisational processes at the
Foulkesian four levels of current, transference, projective, and primor-
dial, so freeing up the organisational mind and allowing it to become
more of a holding and containing organisational matrix. This intervention can be used to treat or prevent what Schwartz (1990) describes as
the psychic life of most organisations akin to a snake pit. In adopting this
method of conducting a group, either over a fixed period or indefinite
period of time, the group analytic approach makes a serious attempt
to get beneath the polished exterior of organisations which often hide
the real pathological dynamics inevitable in any large group process.
Blackwell (1998) describes this potential façade of management as:

> The terminology of excellence, quality, audit, total quality, perfor-
> mance review, evaluation, competency, monitoring, lead bodies etc.
> has a sort of edge to it, an echo of potency, power, control and asser-
> tiveness … . Behind these terms, but hidden by them, lie uncertainty
> and vulnerability which cannot be acknowledged. Thus we have
> a "management speak" that is not a language in the sense that it
> facilitates thought and implicitly recognises the separation and dia-
> lectic between mother and father. It is instead an Orwellian pseudo-
> language which is actually a merging identification with the father
> and his assumed qualities of power, control and assertiveness and
> which is the very denial and annihilation of the Oedipal situation
> and its true creative potential. (p. 542)

This is where a psychoanalytic approach can be most helpful through
getting access to the real variety of psychic lives of an organisation and

so offering a more honest and truthful resolution of difficulties. Here the group analyst is adopting all the usual techniques of developing a matrix through mirroring interventions allowing a free floating discussion, exchange of ideas, and echoing with the leader focusing on being a dynamic administrator and translating unconscious communication into words (Nitsun, 1996). Other contributions have relied on other psychoanalytic conceptual frameworks.

Rice (1965) coined the phrase "primary task" to describe the key activities of an organisation which is most effective when open systems exist. This Tavistock model of organisational human relations (Obholzer & Roberts, 2002) has been the conceptual framework used by many psychoanalytic organisational consultants to explain and understand the complexities of organisational life. Stacey (2001) embeds these ideas within Bion's (1967) work on groups:

> At one level they (people) contribute to its (organisation's) purpose, so constituting a sophisticated (work) group, and at the other level they develop feelings and attitudes about each other, the group and its environment, so constituting a more primitive (basic assumption) group. Both of these models of relating are operative at the same time; when the basic assumption model takes the form of a background emotional atmosphere it may well support the work of the group, but when it predominates it is destructive in the group's work. (p. 97)

In this open system model, permeation within and between different systems is critical to the life of the organisation. If internal systems are operating ineffectively this will affect not only the primary task but also the relation to the external world. Thus, all the more reason to pay serious attention to the intrapsychic and interpersonal processes in any organisation.

One of the main contributions to applying psychoanalysis to organisations is the work of Otto Kernberg. His contribution is focused on the dynamics established in relation to authority in groups and is best summarised in one of his most recent papers (2003):

> As Freud pointed out, the universal nature of Oedipal strivings, the search for and fear of a powerful, protective, dominating

and threatening father image, overshadows the real nature and authority of the leader, and fosters the regression into mass psychology.

However, the more the personality characteristics of the leader reinforce these regressive tendencies, the stronger the tendency for the group or mass to regress along narcissistic or paranoid lines. In earlier work I proposed that, ideally, functional leadership combines the following characteristics:

1. High intelligence, enabling the leader to apply long-range strategic thinking to diagnosing, formulating, communicating and implementing the requirements of the task within its constraints.
2. Sufficient emotional maturity and human depth to be able to assess the personality of others in selecting subordinate leaders and delegating appropriate authority to them.
3. A solid and deep moral integrity that protects the leader from the unavoidable temptations intimately linked to the exercise of power and from the corrupting pressures of the leader's entourage.
4. Sufficiently strong narcissistic tendencies to be able to maintain self-esteem in the face of the unavoidable criticism and attacks of the followers and to avoid depending upon the followers for fulfilment of excessive narcissistic needs.
5. Sufficient paranoid features—in contrast to naiveté—to diagnose early the unavoidable ambivalent and hostile undercurrents in the organisation that express the resentful, rebellious and envious aspects of the aggression directed toward leadership.

> I believe that this is the fundamental paradox of leadership. The narcissistic and paranoid features that, in a certain moderate proportion are its indispensable aspects, are the same characteristics that, at a pathological and exaggerated intensity, will contribute to shifting the task-orientated effects of good leadership into the narcissistic and paranoid mass regression described before. (pp. 692–693)

I will now describe psychoanalytic concepts that highlight the complexities of everyday love and hate that occur in the psychic life of organisations.

## Sexualised feelings in the workplace

Sexualised activities around work are well documented in scandals which appear in the media. Whether it's the "musical beds" of the manager of the England football team or the sexual activities of the president of the United States, sexual feelings and thus acting out are rife in organisations. Here, it is timely to remember the original Oedipal story, which is full of sex and aggression. The impulse to destroy the same sexed rival for the affections of the mother or father is overwhelming. Murderous feelings are rampant and inevitably projected in organisations onto the leader. So what better way to overthrow the leader by either killing him off (same sexed rivalry) or seducing him with sexual favours, so getting rid of the rival?

We know from clinical experience just how difficult erotic transferences can be in the consulting room. Freud originally drew our attention to this powerful transference which has the fundamental wish to seduce the psychoanalytic therapist into a powerful and real sexualised union. Of course, with psychoanalytic work we treat the breaking of this boundary as a cardinal sin; and rightly so, but within organisational life, erotic transferences take on a different quality. The acting out of such powerful affects may indeed signal the ultimate Oedipal triumph by a member of staff wishing to demonstrate sexual prowess. Of course, within organisational life, the psychic reality is also different to the consulting room where individuals may indeed prefer to leave and get married. However, it is critical to differentiate between the acting out of an erotic transference which leaves both individuals dissatisfied and the creation of an alternative coupling in people's lives which may or may not be fulfilling.

### Idealisation of authority

The work of Klein (Segal, 1986; Spillius, 1988a, 1988b) clearly points to the dysfunctional and pathological function of idealisation in human relationships as a way of dealing with feelings of inadequacy and emotional fragility. Clearly located within the paranoid-schizoid position, idealisation and devaluation only serve to maintain a psychic reality that is fundamentally flawed. In other words, seeing the senior manager as having all the answers to the organisation's problems or devaluing his or her contribution which prevents thinking through everyday issues within organisational life. However, both leaders and members of organisations can unwittingly perpetuate this myth to maintain this psychic imbalance. As stated earlier, it was Menzies-Lyth (1988) who first noticed these processes when studying nurse-doctor interactions in hospital settings. Those processes are no less evident in other organisational dynamics. Indeed, many traditional management texts (Covey, 1989) can reinforce this dysfunctional process by suggesting that all the potential power and answers to problems rest in the leader. This power, while real, tends to focus on charismatic and inspirational views of leadership rather than a Bionian and "ordinary" approach to human relations where everyone has good and bad parts and we do our best not to project these into everyone else. For example, in trying to find resolution to a conflict over the allocation of human and financial resources, the manager can either directly provide a solution or allow the staff team to think through the issues and offer a resolution with all group members actively engaged. In traditional management theory the leader often demands idealisation and rarely takes responsibility when things go wrong. Here, unconscious motivations for becoming leaders need to be thoroughly analysed, as authoritarian characteristics can often lead to a dictatorial style which minimises the manager demanding compliance and idealisation from the flock rather than a genuine desire to take forward the primary task of the organisation.

Schwartz (1990) also comments on the pathological aspects of idealisation when questioning the textbook analysis of organisations as operating like "clockwork" in a mechanical way, when in reality, most exist as snake pits where selfishness and narcissism are rife. The promise of the organisational ideal is the achievement of some desired state of perfection which fails to take account of the ordinary hard work that needs to take place for organisations to exist. This is what we read in textbooks which portray an idealised organisation which can prevent a deeper and detailed analysis of what really takes place. He writes:

> The problem is, of course, that while the clockwork organisation is an idea that has great emotional appeal, it does not represent anything that exists in the world, or even that could possibly exist in the world ... . The clockwork organisation has the same problems connected with it as any ego ideal. The ego ideal is formulated as

a response to anxiety and we are driven to pursue it by anxiety. It represents an end to the anxiety that drives toward it. But at its core, our anxiety concerns our finitude, vulnerability and morality, and these are the biological givens of being an organism. We can transcend biology only in fantasy. The clockwork organisation is one of these fantasies. (p. 9)

## Narcissism as a source of destructiveness

As stated earlier in this paper, Kernberg (2003) writes about the healthy narcissism required for a leader to survive organisational life. However, organisations are often populated by excessive narcissistic personality disorders everywhere within the hierarchy.

The implications for organisational psychic life are significant. If both leaders and members of such groups are riddled with pathological narcissism, there emerges a poverty of trust, good faith, and generosity. In Kleinian terminology the paranoid-schizoid position becomes the "normality" of everyday existence. Motives are seen as selfish and personal boundaries are frequently violated, as people do not know where "they finish and the other person begins".

Again, Schwartz (1990) comments on the impact of this American culture within organisational life in analysing the perfectionism he found in NASA:

> In effect: upon NASA had fallen the burden of maintaining the narcissism of a strikingly, and perhaps increasingly narcissistic American culture. Through NASA, Americans were telling themselves that, despite the drubbing the US Army took in Vietnam, despite the fact that American industry could not compete within the American market, much less abroad, despite the fact that many American cities had become modern instantiations of Hobbes' "state of nature"—despite all this America was perfect. This again, is narcissism, but on the level of the whole society. (p. 109)

This particularly destructive form of narcissism involves the mechanism of denial where failings are avoided and allows badness to reside in others to preserve the idealised goodness in one's organisation.

## Envy in organisational life

I have written elsewhere on the role of envy in everyday life in a troubled society (Kapur & Campbell, 2004), describing it as a "terrorist", striking without warning and disappearing with no personal responsibility taken for the trail of destruction left behind on innocent human beings. This process is no less prevalent in everyday organisational life.

Paradoxically, for the organisational leader, envy can be most prevalent when the organisation is successful and people are doing well and feeling well.

Making staff feel good and establishing good morale is a difficult and complex task. Frequently, managers are left frustrated and demoralised when their genuine attempts to make things better are sabotaged. They fail to take into account the powerful role of envy in undermining their best efforts to create a better working life. Hope and trust are frequently spoiled, either because the individual cannot tolerate the vulnerability of accepting goodness or he can feel that the only way to manage impoverishment is to leave the organisation or manager feeling as bad as he does. What can then follow is an impulse to rob the organisation of goodness, so leaving others demoralised by these attacks on the organisational mother; for example, in providing training for staff there are many instances where training opportunities are used to improve the personal CV of staff, to "feather their nest" rather than using training to fulfil both the individual's and organisation's needs. Similarly, managers who envy the talents of their staff will project their inadequacies into their workforce to prevent any rivalry and so "put staff in their place".

I will now describe scenarios where these powerful forces are at work.

## Love or lust?

One of the key ideas behind Bion's (1961) concept of pairing is that two people within a group, male and female, get together in the hope of producing a baby which will produce a messianic leader to overthrow the existing leader of the group, so dealing with the inevitable frustrations in group life. This pairing can be destructive towards the group process by directing efforts away from working through group difficulties and projecting the solution for problems into this idealised and often sexualised pair. Here, it is important to differentiate between the primitive and impulsive emotions of lust versus genuine love and affection, which may also occur in respect of healthy group processes aimed at supporting the leader and the organisation in the fulfilment of its primary task. I will describe an example from another organisation where lust predominated and led to an attack on the group leader.

Confiding sensitive information with colleagues is a difficult decision in teams and organisations as few can predict how good or bad relationships will be in the future. In this particular situation, the senior manager in the department confided to a colleague private information in relation to others. However, this "confidante" soon become displeased at the power and authority that this special relationship gave her boss. She would envy the increasing power of her position. Within the dynamics of this group, this confidante had an opportunity to meet and become close to a male member of staff. Soon, a sexual relationship began and the male colleague become privy to some of the "secrets" held by the senior manager or boss. An attempt was then made to get rid of the boss by this sexualised couple letting others within the team know that their boss was potentially sharing private information with this "special colleague", who was much lower in the management hierarchy than they were. As all of these dynamics evolved and the boss was not overthrown, the sexualised relationship became known to everyone and this pair left the department. The boss survived.

Working together as pairs and couples is inevitable in organisations. This can be for the genuine commitment and "love" of the primary task of the agency or, very powerfully, this can be transformed into destructive lust which is primarily aimed at undermining authority and anarchy. In this example I have tried to highlight how a potentially positive working together to manage the dynamics within a team can be easily hijacked, through envy and jealousy into something much more destructive. This is a fine line in all human relationships, but particularly organisations, where a healthy coupling or pairing can regress into an attack on the group leader. Often, in these lustful and sexualised pairings, there is an acting out of sexual feelings where the opposite sexed member of the pair may really be lusting for the boss, but a subordinate will do, that is, a female member of staff finding the male boss inaccessible and thus having a sexual relationship with someone lower down in the "pecking order" to potentially produce this "new baby" to overthrow the leader who has rejected her advances—a case of a woman scorned!

## All style and no substance

Nitsun (1996) writes:

> I am often reminded of the discrepancy between the organisational
> ideal, the aims and objectives of the organisation, its mission state-
> ments and logical strategies, and the reality of its functioning in
> which conflict, confusion and irrational behaviour abound. (p. 247)

This style of thinking where there is an emphasis on image rather than
outcomes is the norm in most organisations in which people promise
everything but deliver very little. I will describe an experience from my
professional work which highlights this style of human relations.

I will draw upon an incident from my role as chief executive of a
charity. In this new era of a modernised public service all public sector
organisations are faced with the task of combining care with the effi-
cient management of human and financial resources. The values of both
can overlap or be diametrically opposed. The tension in the charity/
voluntary sector is more acute as all charities are limited companies and
by law have to be independently financially viable. This is in contrast to
my experience as a clinical psychologist in the National Health Service
where there is an atmosphere of working with "virtual money": money
that was not real day-to-day revenue.

In both roles there is the potential idealisation of the "command
and control" style of management where a driven and manic leadership style is valued over a more slow and careful analytic style. As a
chief executive it is inevitable that good as well as bad projections make
their way to the top of the hierarchy. This idealisation in organisational
life can manifest itself as the person in authority being endowed with
omnipotence and omniscience, an "all-knowing, all-seeing" boss. It also
may be that if the chief executive is trapped by the power of these projections he may act out these negative processes through a polished and
manic style of management. In looking to colleagues who advocated
a business model of management I found that solutions to problems
were characterised by ruthlessness, whereby all the badness was projected into a situation to justify treating staff as numbers and so permit
acts of cruelty (Brenman, 2006). As a chief executive I have certainly
felt this pull with the temptation to adopt intellectually neat ideas to
justify hate; when there is a financial downturn due to fewer patients in

projects, it is tempting to threaten staff with the loss of their jobs rather than benevolently supporting them to re-establish referral streams.

In the countertransference, when I realised that the idealised implementation of the idealised business model was creating havoc, I attempted to hold on to the positive aspects of the approach which highlights the importance of making sure the primary task of the organisation is to meet the needs of external organisations. However, at the same time I had to recognise the intensity of the tasks against me, so I could apply my psychoanalytic expertise of containing and working through negative processes.

The traditional organisational model of disciplinary and appraisal processes finds it difficult to deal with the powerful unconscious destructive forces at work. Also, and importantly for any manager, distorted transferences, the very stuff of our analytic work, are bound to appear in organisational life. Within any organisation, it is difficult, if not impossible, to highlight the existence of distorted transferences, as staff will rarely see authority figures having the knowledge and expertise to point out their perceptions are incorrect. What often is presented as a legal truth is the result of an advocacy style of discourse rather than one of analytic thinking things through, so increasing the risk that conclusions can be false and not reflect truthful events. This advocacy style forces thoughts and feelings into a discussion of what is the correct interpretation of events, rather than allowing things to be thought through so allowing truth to evolve rather than being forced. It is these potential "babies of lies" achieved through such forceful coupling that can have such bad outcomes. My painful psychic truth is that in idealising the business model I had missed the internal worlds of many people who projected their hatred and envy into the business style as a vehicle to act out destructive attacks. For example, many staff saw the idea of strategically planning services and developments as an attempt to control their individuality and micromanage their professional work, which then allowed staff to attack me as they perceived me to be anti-professional and thus anti-therapeutic. This idealised model legitimised psychotic attacks.

## Organisational mother as the envied object

As Joseph (1986) points out, envy occurs in everyday interactions and organisations are not immune from such processes. As in the clinical situation, people respond to a good and bad breast mother depending on the state of their internal worlds, psychically determined by previous experiences with parental and authority figures. For the manager, the traditional organisational tasks of planning, organising, monitoring, and controlling (Daft & Marcic, 1998) are inevitably contaminated by the intrapsychic histories of individuals.

Pursuing promotion and favour is rife in most organisations and often done by individuals who do little real work and exhibit the manic defences of triumph, control, and contempt so as to achieve what in real terms is often "pseudo success". This particular way of managing work relationships is very common and what can occur is a pseudo compliance with the primary task of the organisation, while the organisation, the maternal object, is being emptied of resources. Staff appraisals and monitoring of progress can feel like being in the room with a false self (Winnicott, 1965), or in Betty Joseph's paper (1981) a staff member who is difficult to reach, that is, not really emotionally engaged with the evaluation process.

This situation is universal in work life where individuals show a dedication to draining resources. In object relations terminology, the bountiful breast is envied and seen as far away from the impoverished state of mind of the member of staff. Anyone relating to the organisation, whether inside or outside it, then feels he can only rob this bountiful mother within a part-object relationship. Often these individuals have a borderline or narcissistic personality so giving the impression of high functioning but in reality they are only superficially engaged with the primary task of the organisation.

The relationship to the organisational mother will depend both on part-object intrapsychic history and on whole object experiences. For example, if individuals have good and full relationships with their parents and significant others, they are less likely to relate to authority in a cold, distant, and greedy manner. If the primary object was experienced as controlling and intrusive then people will relate in a distant and controlling way showing all the signs of manically defending against any real engagement with the organisation. Also, if parental coupling is perverted and unequal, for example if people have parental experiences where one partner was dominant and controlling, individuals will feel they either have to take a submissive or dominant position in relation to management. All of these distorted human relationships will perpetuate basic assumption, anti-work group functioning (Bion, 1961) where pairing, dependency, and fight/flight become the predominant processes within the organisational state of mind. Within the pairing phenomena, relationships will become sexualised with real acting out, so actually producing a baby in reality who is there to take the position of the leader to be overthrown. This may manifest itself in the idealisation of a new member of staff as a "stalking horse" to overthrow the leader. Also, erotic transferences to the leader, which cannot be fulfilled, become reworked on unwitting colleagues.

The envied organisational mother does indeed present a real problem for the impoverished members of any organisation. However, this poses a greater problem for the manager, who, via projective identification, experiences negative feelings and envious attacks from people he is trying to feed. Managers who may genuinely want to help their employees develop their careers are often met with experiences of exploitation aimed at taking resources away from the organisation to pursue selfish ambitions. In my experience of organisational life, whether this be in my previous role as a clinical psychologist and psychotherapist in a hospital or a leader of a voluntary organisation, violent homosexual and heterosexual attacks on both the organisational resources and strengths are rampant. Attacks on linking (Bion, 1961) from the psychotic personality of the member of staff can lead to well intentioned managers either acting out a harsh superego role through disciplinary procedures or collapsing and withdrawing with their morale shattered through trying to generously feed organisational siblings. Table 9 describes my experiences when projections "go mad" and both managers and staff are caught in a vicious cycle of bad internal objects being acted out. It is no coincidence that in running a mental health charity I have felt I was being driven mad, which was aptly described by a dream of one of my secretarial staff, where I had suffered a nervous breakdown. It may be that the primary task of the organisation is to define the characteristics of the destructive phantasies, say in a cancer ward, that the leader gets cancer; in a school, that the headmaster or headmistress fails a regulatory inspection. Here, thought, patience, and careful analysis is overtaken by violent and internally legitimised destructive acts.

Within my own experience, the group matrix became an analysing group process, both formal and informal, the container to understand these processes. I have certainly felt at both ends of the countertransference spectrum, that is, an emptied and a harsh object. While I do not facilitate the staff group, inevitably the projections and transferences

Table 9. When projections go mad!.

| Crazy bosses | Mad staff |
|---|---|
| Might is right (bullying) | Undermining the boss is fun (Oedipal impulse) |
| Do this, do that ... (controlling) | Get you when you're not looking (psychotic attacks) |
| Massage my ego (idealisation) | My job is to make you feel bad (spoiling) |
| Put people in their place (devaluing) | Downsizing the boss (envy) |

will be towards me. Here, as my individual and group psychotherapy training taught me, it is critical to hold on to my therapeutic balance and put words to these emotional demands while ensuring I have enough internal and external support to prevent me acting out with both scenarios: as an emptied object, becoming depressed and as a harsh object, going mad.

## Discussion

I have kept most of the original paper published in 2009 in this chapter. However, in this revised discussion, I wish to make two particular points as to the outcome of an externally facilitated managers group, set up to deal with destructive forces in the organisation and the subsequent issues that have emerged from the Mid-Staffordshire scandal and the Francis Report (2013).

In an attempt to deal with the extremes of "love and hate" so clearly present in our organisation, I established a monthly external group, facilitated by a group analyst. This had mixed results. While it did provide a forum for discussion and an opportunity to reflect on the group matrix of the organisation, it failed to deal with the continued primitive underlying emotional life of the group. Furthermore, the external consultant (as stated in Chapter Seven) had no awareness of the impact of continued destructive processes on the survival of the agency and simply could not be privy to the internal worlds of staff who were using his honest efforts to camouflage their paranoid-schizoid functioning even further. Indeed, to prevent this continued sabotaging of the agency, I had to terminate his group interventions as the external consultant (in the words of one staff member) "was so easily fooled". Further acting out did occur with the reputation of the agency being put at risk by staff contriving to "do their own thing" and totally neglecting the care of the agency, which involved me having to take disciplinary action resulting in dismissal and subsequently, industrial tribunals.

In retrospect, I think having a regular group setting (either internally or externally facilitated) can allow everyone to reflect on and think about psychotic (destructive) and non-psychotic (creative) aspects of group processes. This continues in the agency on a quarterly basis. However, this must occur in tandem with other formal management processes such as clear line management, accountability, and appraisals, otherwise staff can hijack a genuine wish to explore underlying group processes as a way of believing they can control executive decisions and thus have a management responsibility that is out of their remit and authority. This can lead to the unwitting collusion with anti-authority processes that will undermine "depressive position law and order" that are required to keep the agency safe.

As stated at the start of this chapter, the assumption that internal worlds or individual personalities will relate humanely and rationally to the aims and objectives of the agency occurs only randomly and is aptly highlighted by the Mid-Staffordshire scandal and the Francis Report. There, a health agency established to provide good medical care became an organisation delivering such neglect and cruelty that patients lost their lives to staff, by their dehumanisation of patients. Ballat and Campling (2011) attempt to address these issues which are so common in health and social care with their text "Intelligent Kindness", where they suggest maximising kindness from staff to the care of patients can create a "virtuous circle" that produces improved therapeutic alliances and better outcomes. They write:

> Simply put, the more attentively kind staff are, the more their attunement to the patient increases; the more that increases, the more trust is generated; the more trust, the better the therapeutic alliance, the better the outcomes. The result of all this is a reduction in anxiety, improved satisfaction (to staff and patients), less defensiveness and improved conditions for kindness. The suggestion is that, as staff practise more kindly, a virtuous circle is set in motion. (pp. 43–44)

While there are undoubtedly situations where this approach could be effective, I think it may underestimate the primitive emotional forces that were at work in Mid-Staffordshire and in the organisational psychic life of nearly all organisations. Their premise, not unlike the traditional group relations model (Rice, 1965), is that if you intervene to invite staff to think and relate differently there will be a change in how they relate to others that can filter through to their work life, hence transforming cruelty to kindness.

I have not found this to be the case. Indeed, as cited in the organisational examples given, I have found that at best the underlying state of mind is contained and destructive behaviour is inhibited or that temporary "pseudo change" is soon replaced by the original negativity.

In other words, as per the theoretical framework of Chapter One, the paranoid-schizoid functioning and psychotic processes are rarely dissolved. This would be consistent with clinical experience, that the more embedded and chronic the negative state of mind, the more intense and difficult the work becomes (O'Shaughnessy, 2015). In essence the patient or staff member believes they are doing nothing wrong and the abnormal (paranoid-schizoid functioning) becomes normal, rather than the opposite being true, that depressive position functioning becomes normal.

So what is the most helpful intervention? I think the models of change suggested by Ballat and Campling (2011) and the group relations approach (Rice, 1965) are potentially helpful in getting staff to "stop and think" about how they are relating to colleagues and patients. However, in my experience, this is only a temporary change for many staff. Either such interventions have to take place on a recurring basis or they have to be delivered with an awareness that making a permanent change in how staff relate to others is not realistic or attainable. Otherwise, as I have found, assuming patient safety has been protected by such interventions is at best naïve and at worst leads to collusion of pseudo change and poor patient care. Consistent follow-up with such interventions and the use of the "brick mother", disciplinary processes are a necessary reality to maintain patient safety and effective organisational processes.

# CHAPTER NINE

# Employment issues

As stated in Chapter Seven, the world of private practice is very different from the public sector, where employees of an organisation are paid to deliver a service to the patient. In psychoanalytic terminology, there is *always* a third person in the room, employment law. I have found to my own personal and professional cost, that assuming an employee is like a trainee psychotherapist, eager to improve the quality of emotional understanding to the patient, can be a fatal mistake. Rarely, if ever, has this been addressed in the operation of and delivery of therapeutic interventions.

Employment issues fall into two main categories: disciplinary and grievance issues. All have a significant effect on patient care, particularly when you are operating a setting where reliability, consistency, and emotional availability are the essential ingredients of providing an effective and therapeutic atmosphere.

I will describe each of these aspects of employment practice and then speak about the meaning and implications of these for staff, managers, and the overall atmosphere of the organisation.

## Disciplinary

The aim of disciplinary action should be to improve future conduct.
No company should take such action lightly, however, since it can
have serious results for both employer and employee. (ACAS, 1999,
p. 43)

All organisations have a disciplinary procedure based on a three-stage
model of dealing with issues of misconduct:

- A thorough investigation.
- An interview or hearing, giving the employee a chance to hear the
  complaint and put forward his or her side of the matter.
- Making a fair and reasonable decision.

There are generally two levels of breach of conduct: unacceptable or
gross misconduct, which can lead (if there is a case to answer) to either:

- An informal verbal warning.
- A formal verbal warning (which is recorded on file)—in the case of a
  minor offence.
- A formal written warning—for subsequent minor offences or a more
  serious offence.
- A final written warning—for further misconduct. This warning
  would make clear that dismissal may follow if the person fails to
  improve.
- Dismissal—with appropriate notice, will follow if there is insufficient
  improvement or an incident of gross misconduct has occurred, such
  as theft, etc.

So follows the rationale and what appears as a fair procedure to
deal with "bad" behaviour. However, in my experience, this is never
the case. "What belongs to whom" or, in psychoanalytic parlance,
where do the bad parts of the conflict belong, to the employer or the
employee, is a question in a process filled with complexity and "life
and death" issues for the service being delivered. I will give examples
to illustrate the seriousness of the whole process and how if things go
wrong, a service may be extinguished (particularly in the voluntary
sector).

## *Who is the bully?*

This is undoubtedly the biggest question in the workplace when there is any conflict and goes to the heart of most employment disputes. Importantly, within the theoretical framework of this text, it refers to where does the "psychotic personality" belong (Kapur, 2008b)? Using the terminology of the workplace, a bully would have Bion's (1957) four psychotic personality characteristics appearing as:

- An identity suffused with superiority (sadism greater than love).
- An impulsivity, albeit hidden, to put people down (preponderance of destructive impulses).
- A distant relationship with others (a mercurial transference).
- A denial of ordinary issues in the workplace (denial of reality).

A bully/psychotic personality will appear in many guises, some of which are:

- Mr. Nice, hiding Mr. Nasty (manic defences).
- Obsequious, submissive behaviour (inferiority presentation, hiding a superior inner self).
- A loud "pressure of speech" state of mind, not allowing others to speak or creating a feeling in others of "doing something wrong" if they question or explore issues raised with a threat of retribution (massive projective and projective identification processes).

The following situation describes when I, as CEO, was pressured to be the bully and a liar:

> "Contracts within the voluntary agency were under threat as the specifications of staff delivering the services were clearly not being met. This had huge implications for the agency as our reputation as a provider of professional services for severely mentally ill patients was at risk. Clearly this had to be stopped and a correction had to take place to put the appropriate staff in place to deliver the service. I was accused of bullying and victimising staff and making up lies to 'get rid of people' I didn't like."

An investigation, as per our terms and conditions and good employment practice ensued, and I had to take disciplinary action on issues of unacceptable and gross misconduct. Written warnings were issued and a member of staff had to be dismissed.

In many ways, the facts of the situation were "black and white". Unqualified staff were delivering a service to vulnerable people and my responsibility as CEO was to get to the heart of the issue and manage it. However, the storm of projections led to a situation where "particles of psychotic behaviour" took on a life of their own and in the terminology of countertransference reactions, I was an abuser rather than protector of the service (my professional and legal responsibility). Boundaries had to be established for organisational safety. Which is not unlike the characteristics of a "brick mother", referred to in the management of patients who are out of control. In other words, I had to contain the psychotic destructiveness of staff who could not take seriously the damage they were inflicting.

So in employment situations, simple truths from a manager to an employee, or vice versa, can be distorted, to try to justify an attack on the goodness of the person holding the truth. Of course, being an analysand/patient on a couch is very different to being an employee, with the latter not being in a state of mind to discover painful truths about himself in the service of depressive position functioning. While this can be achieved by open and honest discussions, where the truth may emerge after some thought, it rarely occurs where psychic truth becomes intertwined with a legal definition of truth.

So in any disciplinary action, I think it is essential for the manager to know in very simple terms (and as defined in the organisation's terms and conditions) where an act of deceit or misconduct, or a "lie" has taken place. At this point, if the employee "knows" he has "done something wrong", the ordinary process of disciplinary action may flow. However, in the majority of situations, the manager will be exposed to a torrent of projections where he will be portrayed as the bully or liar. As in managing a psychotic transference and for the safety of the patient or organisation, the container has to be strong enough to manage the violent projections of "It's you, rather than me", until the reality or truth of the situation prevails. Otherwise "lies" will be perpetuated, which in organisational life can only lead to festering resentments and ideas of injustice, falsehoods, and poor working relationships.

Edna O'Shaughnessy captures this complex deceitful process when she writes:

How does a patient like M manage in life? Like his objects he constructs a public façade. He disassociates himself internally from his turmoil and skilfully "matches" (his world) externally to what is required of him. Cut off from his depths, his façade is thin and lasts only while relations go smoothly at a superficial level. He soon tends to suspect his object of likewise having a façade, and gets anxious that he is unwanted, is being criticised etc. Projections of acute anxiety begin again and in phantasy, he invades his object to scrutinise its interior and control it to take what he needs from it. The whole cycle of irresolvable, over-involved object relations has begun again, based on a massive projective identification with a lying object in which Mr. M becomes the habitual liar, who is chronically hiding behind and meeting his objects, not with communications, but with lies. (2015, p. 126)

For the psychoanalytic therapist, the task is Herculean to find the truth. For the manager it is near impossible and usually is dealt with by "damage limitation", by restricting the behaviour/role of the liar or involving the above disciplinary processes.

### Grievance

A grievance procedure should provide an open and fair way for employees to make known their complaints, to have those complaints considered by the company to decide whether to accept or reject the complaint. (ACAS, 1999, p. 45)

Companies and employers will have a grievance procedure embedded in their terms and conditions of employment, which usually involves an investigation of a written complaint, followed by informal and formal procedures to resolve the grievance. If a grievance is upheld, disciplinary action may follow if the accused is potentially guilty of misconduct, for example, harassment.

As with the disciplinary process, the grievance process is ripe for projective action and raises the same question in a different way, "Is it you or is it me?"

An example is as follows (and is tragically common if not universal in the early years of senior management).

"A middle manager had clearly been failing to achieve agreed goals in the delivery of her service. After much latitude around time frames, along with 'flexi-time' and 'working from home', simple, but important, activities such as exploring partnerships with statutory providers failed to materialise. Then, out of the blue, a grievance was taken against me of sexual harassment. It came from nowhere, completely knocked me off balance and meant that work for this employee had to be postponed to allow an investigation to take place. She left three months later after these allegations were proved to be false."

If we take seriously that the processes described in Chapter One occur in everyday work relationships, then (particularly if the manager has conducted himself in a thoughtful and careful way, that is, in the depressive position) the launching of a grievance can be one of many things:

– A genuine wish to right a wrong.
– A narcissistic injury from an experience of being slighted, rejected, or persecuted by a manager.
– A murderous Oedipal wish to "kill off" the manager.

I will analyse these grievance dynamics in light of the example above.

## Genuine wish to right a wrong

With employment law, the "third person" in the work setting which comes into analysing any conflict, the idea of a legal truth soon outweighs the psychic truth espoused in the clinical psychoanalytic work described in this text. A legal truth is based on how established legal procedures can uncover tangible objective evidence which points to the guilt or innocence of the accused. Indeed, if these processes were executed in the proper way, many truths would be and are uncovered. However, if the "tangibles" are elicited more through legal processes depending on the characteristics of a particular incident, then real truths rarely emerge. Often legal processes "force" the truth (forced coupling or violent penetration) where the accused is pressurised to accept a piece of behaviour which may or may not be a projection. In the example above, my accusers could and did argue that my monitoring of her work was persecuting and she felt hounded. In a "persecuted, damaged internal world" this would undoubtedly be the case as any demand is experienced as a violent intrusion. Tangible evidence of my monitoring may have proved her case. However, I was very careful to be "orderly and thoughtful" in my style so I was minimising feelings of persecution or harassment. This is where being sure you are adopting a depressive position relational style is critical as then, and only then, can you be sure that the likelihood is that the internal world is reacting in a defensive and disturbing way. So, if a genuine wrong did occur, I could and would apologise as I would be confident that my management was thoughtful and considered. Here, of course, the employee or accusers have to be in the same state of mind for this approach to be successful.

## Narcissistic injury

In the above example, the female employee who was given generous flexibility around time frames for agreed work plans, felt "injured" that I had tightened up on my monitoring of her work, that is, put down a boundary. There are many instances in work life where the placement of boundaries leads to individuals feeling slighted, rejected, and persecuted. This is particularly the case if the individual relates from a paranoid-schizoid state of mind. Boundaries can be experienced as deep emotional injuries and can trigger a whole range of emotions from revenge to retaliation as, in the person's own mind, there is a belief of being attacked.

A grievance then becomes a vehicle for victimhood. Here the destructive narcissism associated with seeking justice leads to the unfolding of complex, prolonged, and negative behaviour, all characteristic of the paranoid-schizoid position (Kapur & Campbell, 2004). Victimhood takes on an identity of its own; the aggrieved person feels justified in pursuing his version of the truth at all costs. For a manager who has behaved reasonably (in the depressive position) this is a nightmare. If boundaries are not established, the employee "does his own thing" and service delivery suffers. This is where the idea of a "negative therapeutic reaction" in management often occurs (Kapur, 2009). It is inevitable in overseeing an orderly and well delivered service that these reactions will occur, as boundaries are essential for good and effective organisational life. Here, the manager has to "know" this will occur (as in clinical work) and manage the event with the overall good of the organisation in mind. Otherwise, patients will suffer from the behaviour and practices of damaging and damaged staff, who are putting their own needs ahead of the service.

## Killing off the manager

> Freud postulated that the growing child's development involves an
> intense struggle with the parent of the same gender and an uncon-
> scious desire to replace the parent. Central to Freud's notion is the
> idea that the child invariably experiences more ordinary feelings
> of competitiveness, hostility and rivalry towards the same sexed
> parent. Although the "complete" Oedipal complex involves strug-
> gles with both parents, the relationship with the parent of the same
> gender is especially at issue. (Stein, 2010, p. 76)

For the purposes of this discussion, I will refer to the same and opposite sexed rivalry with the father figure as it is relevant to the example
cited. Being comfortable with one's own sexuality is part and parcel of
the depressive position. However, in leadership and management, often
female staff do not feel that feminine receptivity is consistent with what is
often perceived as a manly role. Regrettably this can lead to the omnipotence and hostility of the paranoid-schizoid position replacing the more
thoughtful and feminine self, characteristic of the depressive position.

Unfortunately for either the male or female clinician or manager the
containment of complex and often damaged projections are the same.
Frosh (1995) highlights this clinically:

> In the context of the transference, the analyst, whether male or
> female, can be related to as either masculine or feminine, whether
> in terms of "whole object" identity (father or mother) or part object
> attribute (breast, penis), and therefore has to have the capacity to
> tolerate this boundary confusion if the projections of the patient are
> to be understood and ameliorated. (p. 166)

And so to my example. The member of staff presented herself as hostile
and penetrative with an inappropriate use of her sexuality to distort
the reality of events. In other words, while she presented as a "phal-
lic woman", her natural sexuality was hijacked in the service of con-
vincing others of her version of events. The attack on me, in her claim
of harassment was part of this two-pronged strategy to destabilise or
castrate me. In respect of the latter, if we assume she presented with
a male identity, then there was a wish to murder me, take my role to
become the new father figure of the organisation, and couple with the
mother agency. Her murderous attacks were relentless, cunning, and

certainly had all the characteristics of managing patients entrenched in the paranoid-schizoid position (Brenman, 2006; O'Shaughnessy, 2015).

Any manager being on the receiving end of a grievance has to be mindful that he must conduct himself in the depressive position as the likelihood is that a grievance will contain so many damaged parts of the other, that (like a psychoanalytic therapist working his theoretical framework) he has to give himself the best opportunity to consider "what belongs to me and what belongs to you". In a management and leadership role, there is not the comfort and security of a consulting room, with the infrastructure of personal analysis/therapy and clinical supervision. So it is crucial that leaders and managers establish a strong support structure that helps them manage toxic projections that have the added ingredient of employment law. For many managers and leaders the latter can become the "killer blow" as legal truth is valued over psychic truth, where toxic grievances indeed do destroy the recipient. This is particularly the case in industrial tribunals. In my experience industrial tribunals can become the killing fields for many well intentioned leaders, managers, and professionals who want to do the best for their patient, but find that a forceful legal truth is delivered with such penetrative might, that their careers are destroyed. Projections and projective identifications outside the consulting room can cruelly destroy the goodness of those in authority wanting to improve the care of those they look after. An admirable ambition of the depressive position thereby is often thwarted.

In conclusion, managing disciplinary and grievance procedures has to take place within the reality of two powerful processes: tangible, objective, legal evidence and intangible, unconscious, subjective processes. Both will change from moment to moment (PZ $\leftrightarrow$ D) and the unenviable task for any manager is to contain both, so that patients that are looked after are kept safe. As Hanna Segal said in one of her final interviews before her death (Segal, 2008), we can only hope to achieve approximations of the truth:

> The more I think about it … the importance lies in seeking truth, not "The Truth" with a capital T, an omniscience, but truth that is the same as reality. All we are really looking for, in a patient on the couch, is a distinction between lies and truth.

In employment situations, there may only be fragments of the truth which rarely are used for the betterment of both parties.

# CHAPTER TEN

# Conclusion

T his book is born out of the professional reality that contemporary
psychoanalytic ideas are sadly absent in understanding the process of recovery of a severely mentally ill patient. The central idea
behind this book is to apply theoretical concepts and clinical techniques
from a particular psychoanalytic model to understanding the subjective state of mind of people with psychosis. This, along with accepted
good practices in psychiatric care and well-founded research findings,
provides a source of knowledge that I hope will be of help to everyone
working in the real world of public sector provision of services for these
patients. This has been a personal journey for me of hope and despair to
a position of recovery to where this project has proved possible and is
of demonstrable help to patients. This experience of the organisational
psychic life of Threshold is not unlike the personal journey of personal
therapy/analysis in the to and fro movement from the paranoid-schizoid
and depressive positions (Segal, 1986), to the hoped for ultimate "psychic home" where concern for oneself and others eventually predomi-
nates in everyday intrapsychic and interpersonal life.

In this final chapter I want to leave you with an idea that uses one
of the most well known acronyms from my profession of psychology
to capture the essence of the work required by leaders, managers,

clinicians, and staff to create a therapeutic atmosphere conducive to depressive position functioning. In this theoretical framework, rather than IQ referring to intelligence quotient, I would suggest it could be used to refer to "introspective quotient", defined as the *depth* and *breadth* of thinking (alpha processing) required before responding to a projection/projective identification in clinical and organisational life.

In reflecting on the book, I think both dimensions (breadth and depth) are required in all aspects of creating a therapeutic atmosphere, with one dimension being greater than the other according to the characteristics of a particular issue. While the therapeutic community environment models described in Chapter Two do offer considerable breadth in aspects of a residential setting for psychotic patients, I think they could be complemented by the depth of the theoretical model outlined in the Introduction, that is, attending to the internal world of this patient population. Inclusion of this dimension could help staff become more aware of the complexity of the state of mind of the psychotic patient, so maximising the "introspective quotient" of the setting. Chapters Three and Four on group and individual processes clearly require an interpersonal and intrapsychic depth to understand how the patient relates to himself and others. Also, in Chapter Four, "breadth" is required to ensure any individual understanding of the patient is in the context of a well structured and orderly day, with a thought-out care and support plan. In Chapter Five, considerable breadth is required to ensure that training needs are embedded within Maslow's Hierarchy of Needs and in the professional context of mental health and social care requirements.

For research findings, being aware of the breadth of empirically driven guidelines can help the patient emotionally recover from severe mental illness. In inviting any external consultants into the agency (Chapter Seven) it is crucial to consider the context and expertise that they bring into an organisation. Analysing in depth their IQ is critical, as if it's lower than yours or your organisation's, it will lead to damage and chaos that demoralises both managers and staff and ultimately affects patient care. This is also the case in dealing with complex management, leadership, and employment issues (Chapters Eight and Nine).

The IQ of the leader and those in authority will have the most influence on whether therapeutic atmospheres are being created, which bear the characteristics of the depressive position. There will always be paranoid-schizoid functioning in organisational life and the realistic task can only be to lessen this as much as is humanly possible (and to recover from it when it takes place) as there are many complex layers of human relations between externals, leaders, managers, staff, and patients that have to be managed or contained to provide the best chance of the desired outcome, that is, maximising depressive position functioning.

In organisational and clinical life, there are many projective/introjective moments. In clinical practice this is how the psychoanalytic therapist, in this particular framework, responds to a patient's communications. Recently, one of the eminent writers in this area of psychoanalytic practice wrote:

> The chief clinical problem in a dual transference of words and activities beyond words is to enable the patient's predicament to unfold by experiencing both what he conveys by talk and what he conveys by projective identification, while at the same time preventing him from living out his defensive phantasies with the analyst and so using the analysis as a refuge from life instead of a process which leads him to a fuller resumption of his own life. (O'Shaughnessy, 2015, p. 81)

A high IQ, in this theoretical context, is characterised by always paying attention to:

- Who is doing what to whom?
- Who is putting what into whom and is it good or bad?
- Is it me or is it you?

In creating a therapeutic atmosphere this has to occur within the context of how the individual is functioning in a mental health, housing, and social care context. Critically, to maximise depressive position functioning, every projective moment (as in the consulting room) is worthy of attention and requires considerable "alpha processing" to understand the true nature of the state of mind (paranoid-schizoid or depressive), and then to formulate an introjective response which maximises depressive position functioning. In the overall organisational system, particularly in the voluntary sector, there are crucial "executive introjective moments" (see Chapter Seven) which can dictate the life or death of an agency. In other statutory settings, where funding is not omnipresent, these moments still occur and do affect the quality of the therapeutic atmosphere being created, rather than its very existence. Here, as stated consistently in this text, the pressure to act out (retaliate or collapse) is enormous and thus those in this position require a preponderance of good internal and external objects to survive and flourish.

In concluding this text, I will go back to my patient that I met thirty years ago. Managerially, clinically, and empirically what would I have liked to provide for her? Managerially, a safe, secure, physical setting, characterised by order, firm boundaries, and individualised care, where her needs (physical and emotional) could be met under the leadership of someone displaying a serious understanding of her condition. Concern, thought, with a touch of humility are the qualities needed in the clinician for those in his care; the opposite of destructive narcissism.

Clinically, I would like to offer a setting where she would be quietly and thoughtfully listened to over a long period of time, in a consistent and reliable way, where all her communications are understood and contained, individually and in a group. I would like thoughtfully delivered group experiences to let her know she can receive some relief from the feelings of isolation and the stigma of mental illness. By knowing there are others in the same boat and she is not alone with her madness.

Empirically, I would like to know that she gets better. While I can't prove this in the "cause and effect" way, at the very least I can know that something in the atmosphere I have provided has helped her recover from one of the most devastating illnesses, psychosis. I hope in Threshold, some of this has been achieved for the majority of patients we have looked after in the last twenty-five years.

# REFERENCES

ACAS (1999). *Employing People*. Plymouth, UK: Latimer Trend.

Alexander, F., & French, T. (1946). *Psychoanalytic Therapy: Principles and Applications*. New York: Ronald Press.

Azim, H. F. A., Piper, W., Segal, P. M., Nixon, C. W. H., & Duncan, S. C. (1991). The quality of object relations scale. *Bulletin of the Messinger Clinic, 55*: 323–343.

Ballat, J., & Campling, P. (2011). *Intelligent Kindness: Reforming the Culture of Healthcare*. London: Royal College of Psychiatrists.

Becker, M., Diamond, R., & Sainfort, F. (1993). A new patient focused index for measuring quality of life in persons with severe and persistent mental illness. *Quality of Life Research, 3*: 239–251.

Beecham, J., & Knapp, M. (1992). Costing psychiatric interventions. In: C. Thornicroft, C. Bercon, & J. Wing (Eds.), *Measuring Mental Health*. London: Gaskell.

Bentall, R. P. (2004). *Madness Explained*. London: Penguin.

Berke, J. (1980). Therapeutic community models in Kingsley Hall. In: E. Jansen (Ed.), *The Therapeutic Community*. London: Croom Helm.

Berke, J. H., Mascoliner, C., & Ryan, T. J. (1995). *Sanctuary: The Arbour Experience of Community Care*. London: Process Press.

Betcher, R. W. (1983). The treatment of depression in brief inpatient group psychotherapy. *International Journal of Group Psychotherapy, 33*: 365–385.

Bion, W. R. (1957). Differentiation of the psychotic from the non-psychotic personalities. In: Bion, W. R. (1967), *Second Thoughts* (pp. 43–64). London: Karnac.

Bion, W. R. (1959). Attacks on linking. In: Bion, W. R. (1967), *Second Thoughts* (pp. 93–109). London: Karnac.

Bion, W. R. (1961). *Experiences in Groups.* New York: Basic Books.

Bion, W. R. (1962). *Learning from Experience.* London: Karnac.

Blackwell, D. (1998). A response to Psychoanalysis and the Politics of Organisational Theory: comment on article by Andrew Cooper. *Group Analysis, 31*: 296–303.

Bola, J. R., & Mosher, L. R. (2003). Treatment of acute psychoses without neuroleptics: Two-year outcomes from the Sotiria Project. *Journal of Nervous & Mental Disease, 191*: 219–229.

Bowlby, J. (1988). *A Secure Base: Clinical Implications of Attachment Theory.* London: Routledge.

Boyle, M. (2002). *Schizophrenia: A Scientific Delusion? (2nd ed.).* New York: Routledge.

Brabender, V. M. (1985). Time-limited inpatient group therapy: A developmental model. *International Journal of Group Psychotherapy, 35*: 373–390.

Breier, A., & Strauss, J. S. (1987). The role of social relationships in the recovery from psychotic disorders. *American Journal of Psychiatry, 141*: 947–955.

Brenman, E. (1985). Cruelty and narrow-mindedness. *International Journal of Psychoanalysis, 66*: 273–281. Reprinted in E. Bott Spillius (Ed.), *Melie Klein Today: Developments in Theory & Practice, Vol. 1, Mainly Theory* (pp. 256–271). London: Routledge, 1988.

Brenman, E. (2006). *Recovery of the Lost Good Object.* London: Routledge.

British Psychological Society/Division of Clinical Psychology (2013). *Classification of Behaviour and Experience in Relation to Functional Psychiatric Diagnoses: Time for a Paradigm Shift.*

Britton, R. (1989). The missing link: parental sexuality in the Oedipus complex. In: R. Britton, M. Feldman, & E. O'Shaughnessy (Eds.), *The Oedipus Complex Today: Clinical Implications* (pp. 83–101). London: Karnac.

Britton, R., & Steiner, J. (1994). Interpretation: Selected fact or overvalued idea? *International Journal of Psychoanalysis, 75*: 1069–1078.

Brockhoven, T. (1963). *Moral Treatment in American Psychiatry.* New York: Springer.

Brown, S., Barraclough, B., & Inskip, H. (2000). Causes of the excess mortality of schizophrenia. *British Journal of Psychiatry, 177*: 212–217.

Budman, S. H. (1981). Significant treatment factors in short-term group psychotherapy. *Group, 5*: 25–31.

Campling, P. (2004). A psychoanalytic understanding of what goes wrong: the importance of projection. In: P. Campling, S. Davies, & G. Farquharson (Eds.), *From Toxic Institutions to Therapeutic Environments* (pp. 32–44). London: Gaskell.

Campling, P., Davies, S., & Farquharson, G. (Eds.) (2004). *From Toxic Institutions to Therapeutic Environments: Residential Settings in Mental Health Services.* London: Gaskell.

Chiesa, M., Fonagy, P., & Holmes, J. (2004). An experimental study of treatment outcome: the Cassel-Devon Personality Disorder Project. In: J. Lees, N. Manning, D. Menzies, & N. Morant (Eds.), *A Culture of Enquiry—Research Evidence and The Therapeutic Community* (pp. 205–217). London: Jessica Kingsley.

Connolly, M. B., Crits-Christoph, P., Shappel, S., Barter, J. P., Luborsky, L., & Shaffer, C. (1999). Relation of transference interpretations to outcome in the early sessions of brief supportive-expressive psychotherapy. *Psychotherapy Research, 9*: 485–495.

Cook, T. D., & Campbell, D. T. (1979). *Field Quasi-experimentation: Design and Analysis for Settings.* Chicago, IL: Rand McNally.

Cooper, D. (1986). *Psychiatry and Anti-Psychiatry.* London: Tavistock.

Cory, T. R., & Page, D. (1978). Group techniques for reflecting change in the more disturbed patient. *Group, 2*: 149–155.

Covey, P. (1989). *The 7 Habits of Highly Effective People.* Sydney, Australia: Simon & Schuster.

Daft, R. L., & Marcic, D. (1998). *Understanding Management (2nd ed.).* Orlando, FL: Dryden Press.

Davies, S., & Abbot, P. (2007). Forensic Rehabilitation, in: Roberts, G., Davenport, S., Holloway, F., & Tattan, T., *Enabling Recovery and Practice of Rehabilitation Psychiatry.* (pp. 351–368), London: Gaskell, Royal College of Psychiatrists.

Derogatis, L. R. (1983). *SCL-90-R. Administration, Scoring and Procedures Manual II for the Revised Version.* Towson, MD: Clinical Psychometric Research.

Dewey, J. (1933). *How We Think.* Boston, MA: Heath.

Diamond, R., & Becker, M. (1999). The Wisconsin Quality of Life Index: A multidimensional model for measuring quality of life. *Journal of Clinical Psychiatry, 60*: 29–31.

Donnelly, M., McGilloway, S., Mays, N., Knapp, M., Kavanagh, S., Beecham, J., Fenyo, A., & Astin, J. (1996). Leaving hospital, one- and two-year outcomes of long-stay psychiatric patients discharged to the community. *Journal of Mental Health, 5*: 245–255.

Endicott, J., Spitzer, R. L., Fleiss, J. L., & Cohen, J. (1976). The Global Assessment Scale—A procedure for measuring overall severity of psychiatric disturbance. *Archives of General Psychiatry, 33*: 766–771.

Eraut, M. (2012). Developing a broader approach to professional learning. In: A. McKee & M. Eraut (Eds.), *Learning Trajectories, Innovation and Identity for Professional Development* (pp. 21–45). London: Springer.

Fairbairn, W. R. D. (1952). *Psychoanalytic Studies of the Personality*. London: Routledge.

Foulkes, S. H. (1964). *Therapeutic Group Analysis*. London: Karnac, 1984.

Francis, R. (2015). *Report of the Mid-Staffordshire NHS Foundation Trust Public Inquiry. Executive Summary*. London: The Stationary Office.

Frank, J. D. (1959). *Persuasion and Healing*. Baltimore, MD: Johns Hopkins University Press.

Fromm-Reichmann, F. (1950). *Principles of Intensive Psychotherapy*. Chicago, IL: University of Chicago Press.

Frosh, S. (1995). Masculine mastery and fantasy, or the measuring of the phallus. In: A. Elliott & S. Frosh (Eds.), *Psychoanalysis in Contexts* (pp. 166–187). London: Routledge.

George, C., Kaplan, N., & Main, M. (1985). *The Adult Attachment Interview*. Berkeley, CA: Department of Psychology, University of California at Berkeley.

Gomez, L. (1989). *An Introduction to Object Relations*. London: Free Association.

Greene, L. R., & Cole, M. B. (1991). Level and form of psychopathology and the structure of group therapy. *International Journal of Group Psychotherapy, 41*: 499–521.

Grinberg, N., Sor, D., & Debianchedi, E. T. (1975). *Introduction to the Work of Bion*. Blairgowrie, UK: Clunie Press.

Grotstein, J. S. (1979). Demoniacal possession, splitting and the torment of joy: A psychoanalytic inquiry into the negative therapeutic, reaction, unanalyzability and psychotic states. *Contemporary Psychoanalysis, 15*: 407–445.

Haigh, R. (2007). The new day TC's. Five radical features. *Therapeutic Communities, 28*: 111–126.

Haigh, R. (2013). The quintessence of a therapeutic environment. *Therapeutic Communities: The International Journal of Therapeutic Communities, 34*: 615.

Harris, E. E., & Barraclough, B. (1998). Excess mortality of mental disorder. *British Journal of Psychiatry, 175*: 11–53.

Heimann, P. (1950). On counter-transference. *International Journal of Psychoanalysis, 31*: 81–84.

Heimann, P. (1956). Dynamics of transference interpretations. *International Journal of Psychoanalysis, 37*: 303–310.

Hill, C. E. (1978). Development of a counsellor verbal response category system. *Journal of Counselling Psychology, 25*: 461–468.

Hobson, R. P. (2013). *Consultations in Psychoanalytic Psychotherapy*. London: Karnac.

Hobson, R. P., & Kapur, R. (2005). Working in the transference: Clinical and research perspectives. *Psychology and Psychotherapy: Theory, Research and Practice, 78*: 1–21.

Hobson, R. P., Patrick, M., Kapur, R., & Lyons-Ruth, K. (2013). Research reflections. In: R. P. Hobson (Ed.), *Consultations in Psychoanalytic Psychotherapy* (pp. 183–203). London: Karnac.

Hobson, R. P., Patrick, M. P. H. C., & Valentine, N. Q. (1998). Objectivity in psychoanalytic judgements. *British Journal of Psychiatry, 173*: 172–177.

Holloway, F. (2007). Putting it all together—the care programme at its best. In: G. Roberts, S. Davenport, F. Holloway, & T. Tattan (Eds.), *The Principles and Practice of Rehabilitation Psychiatry*. London: Gaskell/Royal College of Psychiatrists.

Horowitz, M. J. (1987). *States of Mind: Analysis of Change in Psychotherapy*. New York: Plenum.

Hovarth, A. O., & Greenberg, L. S. (1994). *The Working Alliance: Theory, Research & Practice*. New York: J. Wiley & Sons.

Isaacs, S. (1952). The nature and function of phantasy. In: M. Klein, P. Heimann, S. Isaacs, & J. Riviere (Eds.), *Developments in Psychoanalysis* (pp. 67–121). London: Karnac.

Jackson, M. (2001). *Weathering the Storms: Psychotherapy for Psychosis*. London: Karnac.

Jansen, E. (Ed.) (1980). *The Therapeutic Community*. London: Croom Helm.

Johnstone, L., & Ballos, R. (2006). *Formulation in Psychology and Psychotherapy: Making Sense of People's Problems*. London: Routledge.

Jones, M. (1964). *Social Psychiatry in Practice: The Idea of a Therapeutic Community*. London: Penguin.

Jones, M. (1968). *Beyond the Therapeutic Community: Social Learning and Psychiatry*. London: Yale University Press.

Joseph, B. (1975). The patient who is difficult to reach. Reprinted in: E. Bott Spillius (Ed.), *Melanie Klein Today: Developments in Theory & Practice, Vol. 2, Mainly Practice* (pp. 48–60). London: Routledge, 1988.

Joseph, B. (1981). Towards the experiencing of psychic pain. In: J. S. Grotstein (Ed.), *Do I Dare Disturb the Universe? A Memorial to Wilfred R. Bion* (pp. 94–102). Beverley Hills, CA: Caesura Press.

Joseph, B. (1986). Envy in everyday life. In: M. Feldman & E. Bott Spillius (Eds.), *Psychic Equilibrium and Psychic Change* (pp. 181–191). London: Routledge.

Kane, M. (2012). "Knowing (and not knowing) one's place", organisational ranking and the operation of envy and shame in organisational life. *Organisational & Social Dynamics, 12*: 194–209.

Kapur, R. (1987). Depression: An integration of T.A. and psychodynamic concepts. *Transactional Analysis Journal, 17*: 345–350.

Kapur, R. (1991). Projective processes in psychiatric hospital settings. *Melanie Klein & Object Relations, 9*: 16–25.

Kapur, R. (1993). The effects of group interpretations with severely mentally ill patients. *Group Analysis, 26*: 411–432.

Kapur, R. (1998). *The Effects of Interpretation on the State of Mind of the Patient in Individual Psychotherapy.* Unpublished PhD thesis, Birkbeck College, University of London.

Kapur, R. (1999). Clinical interventions in group psychotherapy. In: V. L. Schermer & M. Pines (Eds.), *Group Psychotherapy of the Psychoses* (pp. 260–298). London: Jessica Kingsley.

Kapur, R. (2001). Omagh: the beginning of the reparative impulse. *Psychoanalytic Psychotherapy, 15*: 265–278. Also in: C. Covington, P. Williams, J. Avondale, & J. Knox (Eds.), *Terrorism and War: Unconscious Dynamics of Political Violence* (pp. 315–328). London: Karnac, 2002.

Kapur, R. (2005). Dealing with damage: The desire for psychic violence to soothe psychic pain. *Psychotherapy & Politics International, 3*: 180–193.

Kapur, R. (2008a). Kali: The Indian goddess of destruction and containing castration impulses in groups. *Group, 32*: 35–43.

Kapur, R. (2008b). Applying Bion's concept of psychotic personality to staff and patients. In: J. Gale, A. Realpe, & E. Pedriali (Eds.), *Therapeutic Communities for Psychosis* (pp. 52–62). Hove, UK: Routledge.

Kapur, R. (2009). Managing primitive emotions in organisations. *Group Analysis, 42*: 31–46.

Kapur, R. (2014). As a NASTY clinical psychologist am I statistically (professionally) insignificant? *Clinical Psychology Forum, 255*: 47–49.

Kapur, R., & Campbell, J. (2004). *The Troubled Mind of Northern Ireland: an Analysis of the Emotional Effects of the Troubles.* London: Karnac.

Kapur, R., Miller, K., & Mitchell, E. (1988). A comparison of therapeutic factors within in-patient and out-patient psychotherapy groups. Implications for therapeutic techniques. *British Journal of Psychiatry, 152*: 229–233.

Kapur, R., Ramage, L., & Waller, K. (1986). Group psychotherapy in an inpatient setting. *Psychiatry, 49*: 362–349.

Kapur, R., Weir, M. B., McKevitt, C., Devine, M., Collins, L., Maxwell, H., & Heaney, C. (1997). An evaluation of Threshold therapeutic communities in Northern Ireland. *Irish Journal of Psychological Medicine, 14*: 65–68.

Karterud, S. (1988a). What are the prerequisites and indications of the therapeutic community proper?: a comparative study. *Acta Psychiatrica Scandinavica, 77*: 658–669.

Karterud, S. (1988b). The valence theory of Bion and the significance of DSM-III diagnoses for in-patient behaviour. *Acta Psychiatrica Scandinavica*, 78: 462–470.

Karterud, S. (1989). A comparative study of six different groups with respect to their basic assumption functioning. *International Journal of Group Psychotherapy*, 39: 355–376.

Kennard, D. (2008). A view of the evolution of therapeutic communities for people suffering from psychosis. In: *Therapeutic Communities for Psychosis* (pp. 3–15). London: Routledge.

Kernberg, O. F. (1976). *Object Relations Theory and Clinical Psychoanalysis*. New York: Jason Aronson.

Kernberg, O. F. (1980). *Ideology, Conflict and Leadership in Groups and Organisations*. New Haven, CT: Yale University Press.

Kernberg. O. F. (2003). Sanctioned social violence: A psychoanalytic view, Part II. *International Journal of Psychoanalysis*, 84: 683–689.

Killaspy, H., Martson, L., Omar, R. Z., Green, N., Harrison, I., Lean, M., Holloway, F., Craig, T., Leavey, G., & King, M. (2013). Service quality and clinical outcomes: an example from mental health rehabilitation services in England. *British Journal of Psychiatry*, 202: 28–34.

Kinderman, P. (2014). *A Prescription for Psychiatry: Why We Need a Whole New Approach to Mental Health and Well-being*. London: Palgrave Macmillan.

Kingdon, D. (1994). Core programme approach. Recent government policy and legislation. *Psychiatric Bulletin*, 18: 68–70.

Klein, M. (1933). The early development of conscience in the child. In: *Love, Guilt and Reparation and other Works, 1921–1925* (pp. 248–257). London: Vintage, 1988.

Klein, M. (1946). Notes on some schizoid mechanisms. *International Journal of Psychoanalysis*, 22: 99–110. Also in: Mitchell, J. (Ed.), *The Selected Melanie Klein* (pp. 175–200). New York: Free Press, 1986.

Klein, M. (1952a). The origins of transference. *International Journal of Psychoanalysis*, 33: 433–438. Also in: Mitchell, J. (Ed.), *The Selected Melanie Klein* (pp. 201–210). New York: Free Press, 1986.

Klein, M. (1952b). The origins of transference. In: *Envy and Gratitude and Other Works, 1946–1963* (pp. 48–56). London: Vintage, 1997.

Klein, M. (1957). Envy and gratitude. In: *Envy and Gratitude and Other Works, 1946–1963* (pp. 176–235). London: Vintage, 1997.

Klein, M. (1959). Our adult world and its roots in infancy. In: *Envy and Gratitude and Other Works, 1946–1963* (pp. 247–263). London: Vintage, 1997.

Klein, R. H. (1977). In-patient group psychotherapy: Practical considerations and special problems. *International Journal of Group Psychotherapy, 27*: 101–114.

Laing, R. D. (1967). *The Politics of Experience*. New York: Ballantine.

Lefevre, D. (1994). The power of counter-transference in groups for the severely mentally ill: special section—Group analysis and the psychoses. *Group Analysis, 27*: 441–447.

Leff, J. (Ed) (1997). *Care in the Community—Illusion or Reality?* Chichester, UK: J. Wiley & Sons.

Leff, J. (2014). Voices. *British Journal of Psychiatry, 204*: 162.

Leff, J., & Trieman, N. (2000). Long-stay patients discharged from psychiatric hospitals, social and clinical outcomes after five years in the community. The TAPS Project 46. *British Journal of Psychiatry, 176*: 217–223.

Leszcz, M., Yalom, I. D., & Norden, M. (1985). The value of inpatient group psychotherapy: Patients' perceptions. *International Journal of Group Psychotherapy, 35*: 411–433.

Lewis, C. S. (1946). *The Great Divorce*. London: Fount Paperbacks, 1983.

Lopez-Corvo, R. E. (2003). *The Dictionary of the Work of W. R. Bion*. London: Karnac.

Lucas, R. (2009). *The Psychotic Wavelength: A Psychoanalytic Perspective for Psychiatry*. Hove, UK: Routledge.

Marcovitz, R. J., & Smith, J. E. (1983). Patients' perceptions of curative factors in short-term group psychotherapy. *International Journal of Group Psychotherapy, 33*: 21–39.

Maslow, A. (1954). *Motivation and Personality*. New York: Harper & Row.

McKee, A., & Eraut, M. (Eds.) (2012). *Learning Trajectories, Innovation and Identity for Professional Development*. Springer: London.

Menninger, K. (1959). *A Psychiatrist's World: The Selected Papers of Karl Menninger*. New York: Viking.

Menzies-Lyth, I. (1988). *Containing Anxiety in Institutions. Selected Essays Volume 1*. London: Free Association.

Moos, R. H. (1996a). *Community Oriented Programs Environment Scale Manual (3rd ed.)*. Palo Alto, CA: Mind Garden.

Moos, R. H. (1996b). *Ward Atmosphere Scale (3rd ed.)*. Redwood City, CA: Mind Garden.

Moos, R. H. (1997). *Evaluating Therapeutic Environments: The Quality of Psychiatric and Substance Abuse Programmes*. New Brunswick, NJ: Transaction.

Mosher, L. R. (2004). Non-hospital, non-drug intervention with first episode psychosis. In: J. Read, L. R. Mosher, & R. P. Bentall (Eds.), *Models of Madness*. London: Brunner-Routledge.

Mosher, L. R., Pollin, W., & Stabenernau, J. R. (1971). Identical twins discordant for schizophrenia: Neurologic findings. *Archives of General Psychiatry, 24*: 422–430.

National Mental Health Unit (2010). In: www.enablingenviroments.com, p. 19.

Nitsun, M. (1988). Early development: Linking the individual and the group. *Group Analysis, 22*: 249–260.

Nitsun, M. (1996). *The Anti-Group Destructive Forces in the Group and Their Creative Potential*. London: Routledge.

Obholzer, A., & Roberts, V. S. (2002). *The Unconscious at Work: Individual and Organisational Stress in the Human Services*. Hove, UK: Brunner-Routledge.

Ogden, T. (2010). Why read Fairbairn? *International Journal of Psychoanalysis, 91*: 101–118. Orlando, FL: Harcourt Press.

O'Neill, T., & Wells, B. (2015). Bridging the gap: A model for facilitating mainstream psychological and mental health service provision for socially excluded people with complex needs. *Clinical Psychology Forum, 205*: 31–41.

Opalic, P. (1989). Existential and psychopathological evaluation of group psychotherapy of neurotic and psychotic patients. *International Journal of Group Psychotherapy, 39*: 389–411.

O'Shaughnessy, E. (2015). Can a liar be psychoanalysed? In: *Enquiries in Psychoanalysis: Collected Papers of Edna O'Shaughnessy* (pp. 118–132). London: Routledge.

Overall, J. E., & Gorham, D. R. (1962). The brief psychiatric rating scale. *Psychological Reports, 10*: 799–812.

Pappas, D., Yannitsi, S., & Liakos, S. (1997). Therapeutic communities: Evaluation of in-patient groups in a general psychiatric unit. *International Journal for Therapeutic and Supportive Organisations, 18*: 285–296.

Pedriali, E. (1997). Italian therapeutic communities: from historical analysis to hypotheses for change. *Therapeutic Communities, 18*: 3–13.

Pekala, R. J., Siegal, J. M., & Ferrar, D. M. (1985). The problem solving support group: Structured group therapy for psychiatric in-patients. *International Journal of Group Psychotherapy, 35*: 391–410.

Perry, J. W. (1974). *The Far Side of Madness*. Englewood Cliffs, NJ: Prentice-Hall.

Pines, M. (2000). *Bion and Group Psychotherapy*. London: Jessica Kingsley.

Piper, W. E., Joyce, A. S., McCollum, M., & Azim, H. F. A. (1993). Concentration and correspondence of transference interpretations in short-term psychotherapy. *Journal of Consulting and Clinical Psychology, 61*: 586–595.

Plutchik, R. (2000). *Emotions in the Practice of Psychotherapy*. Washington, DC: American Psychological Association.

Plutchik, R., & Kellerman, H. (1974). *Manual for the Emotions Profile Index*. Los Angeles, CA: Western Psychological Services.

Profita, J., Correy, N., & Klein, F. (1989). Sustained, multimodal out-patient group therapy for chronic psychotic patients. *Hospital and Community Psychiatry, 40*: 943–946.

Ralph, R. S., & Corrigan, P. G. (Eds.) (2005). *Recovery in Mental Illness: Broadening Our Understanding of Wellness*. Washington, DC: American Psychological Association.

Rappaport, R. N. (1960). *Community as Doctor*. London: Tavistock.

Rice, A. K. (1965). *Learning for Leadership*. London: Tavistock.

Rice, C., & Rutan, S. (1997). *Inpatient Group Psychotherapy: A Psychodynamic Approach*. New York: Macmillan.

Riesenberg-Malcolm, R. (1986). Interpretation, the past in the present. In: E. Bott Spillius (Ed.), *Melanie Klein Today: Developments in Theory & Practice, Vol. 2, Mainly Practice* (pp. 73–89). London: Routledge, 1988.

Roberts, G., Davenport, S., Holloway, F., & Tattan, T. (Eds.) (2006). *Enabling Recovery: The Principles and Practice of Rehabilitation Psychiatry*. London: Gaskell/Royal College of Psychiatrists.

Rogers, C. R. (1951). *Client-centred Therapy*. Boston, MA: Houghton-Mifflin.

Rosen, A., Hadzi-Povlowic, D., & Parker, G. (1989). The life skills profile: A measure assessing function and disability in schizophrenia. *Schizophrenia Bulletin, 15*: 325–357.

Rosenfeld, H. R. (1971a). A clinical approach to the psychoanalytic theory of life and death instincts: An investigation into the aggressive aspects of narcissism In: E. Bott Spillius (Ed.), *Melanie Klein Today: Developments in Theory & Practice, Vol. 1, Mainly Theory* (pp. 239–255). London: Routledge 1988.

Rosenfeld, H. R. (1971b). Contribution to the psychopathology of psychotic states: the importance of projective identification in the ego structure and the object relations of the psychotic patient. In: E. Bott Spillius (Ed.), *Melanie Klein Today: Developments in Theory & Practice, Vol. 1, Mainly Theory* (pp. 117–137). London: Routledge, 1988.

Rosenfeld, H. R. (1987). *Impasse and Interpretation: Therapeutic and Antitherapeutic Factors in the Psychoanalytic Treatment of Psychotic, Borderline and Neurotic Patients*. London: Brunner-Routledge.

Ryff, C. D. (1989). Happiness is everything, or is it? Explorations on the meaning of psychological well-being. *Journal of Personality and Social Psychology, 57*: 1–13.

Sackett, D. L., Rosenberg, W. M. C., Groy, J. A. M., Hernes, C. B., & Richardson, W. S. (1996). Evidence based medicine: what it is and what it isn't. *British Medical Journal, 312*: 71–72.

Schaffer, N. D. (1982). Multidimensional measures of therapist behaviour as predictors of outcome. *Psychological Bulletin, 92*: 670–681.

Schon, D. A. (1983). *The Reflective Practitioner*. London: Temple Smith.

Schwartz, H. S. (1990). *Narcissistic Process and Corporate Decay: The Theory of the Organisational Ideal*. New York: New York University Press.

Segal, H. (1981). *The Work of Hanna Segal: A Kleinian Approach to Clinical Practice*. London: Free Association.

Segal, H. (1986). *Introduction to the Work of Melanie Klein*. London: Hogarth.

Segal, H. (2008). The queen of darkness. *The Guardian* newspaper, September 8.

Shapiro, E. R. (2001). Institutional learning as a chief executive. In: L. J. Gould, L. F. Stapley, & M. Stein (Eds.), *The Systems Psychodynamics of Organisations* (pp. 175–196). New York: Karnac.

Shrout, P. E., & Fleiss, J. L. (1979). Intra-class correlations. Uses in assessing rater reliability. *Psychological Bulletin, 86*: 420–428.

Sinason, M. (1993). Who is the mad voice inside? *Psychoanalytic Psychotherapy, 7*: 287–321.

Sinason, M., & Richards, J. (2014). The internal cohabitation model. *British Journal of Psychotherapy, 32*: 314–327.

Slade, M. (2009). *Personal Recovery and Mental Illness: A Guide for Mental Health Professionals*. Cambridge: Cambridge University Press.

Sohn, L. (1985). Narcissistic organisation, projective identification and the formation of the identificate. In: E. Bott Spillius (Ed.), *Melanie Klein Today: Developments in Theory & Practice, Vol. 1, Mainly Theory* (pp. 271–292). London: Routledge, 1988.

Sokis, D. A. (1970). A brief follow-up rating. *Comprehensive Psychiatry, 11*: 445–459.

Spillius, E. Bott (1988a). *Melanie Klein Today: Developments in Theory & Practice, Vol. 1, Mainly Theory*. London: Routledge.

Spillius, E. Bott (1988b). *Melanie Klein Today: Developments in Theory & Practice, Vol. 2, Mainly Practice*. London: Routledge.

Spitzer, W. O., Dobson, A. J., Hall, J., Chesterman, E., Levi, J., Shepherd, R., Battista, R. N., & Catchlove, B. R. (1981). Measuring the quality of life of cancer patients. A concise QL-index for use by physicians. *Journal of Chronic Diseases, 34*: 585–597.

Stacey, R. (2001). Complexity at the "edge" of the basic assumption group. In: L. J. Gould, L. F. Stapley, & U. Stein (Eds.), *The Systems Psychodynamics of Organisations* (pp. 91–114). London: Karnac.

Stapley, L. F. (1996). *The Personality of the Organisation: A Psycho-Dynamic Explanation of Culture and Change*. London: Free Association.

Stein, M. (2010). Oedipus Rex at Enron: leadership, Oedipal struggles and organisational collapse. In: H. Brunning & M. Perini (Eds.), *Psychoanalytic Perspectives on a Turbulent World* (pp. 65–92). London: Karnac.

Steiner, J. (1993). *Psychic Retreats: Pathological Organisations of the Personality in Psychotic, Neurotic and Borderline Patients.* London: Routledge.

Steiner, J. (2012). *Seeing and Being Seen: Emerging from a Psychic Retreat.* London: Routledge.

Strachey, J. (1934). The nature of the therapeutic action of psychoanalysis. *International Journal of Psychoanalysis, 15*: 127–159.

Strupp, H. H. (1970). Specific versus unspecific factors in psychotherapy and the problem of control. *Archives of General Psychiatry, 23*: 393–407.

Sullivan, H. S. (1962). *Schizophrenia as a Human Process.* New York: W. W. Norton.

Timko, C., & Moos, R. H. (1998). Determinants of the treatment climate in psychiatric and substance abuse programmes. *Journal of Substance Abuse, 7*: 3–59.

Trieman, N., & Leff, J. (2002). Long-term outcome of long-stay psychiatric in-patients considered unsuitable to live in the community. TAPS Project 44. *British Journal of Psychiatry, 181*: 428–432.

Tuke, S. (1813). *Description of the Retreat.* London: Process Press, 1996.

Tyler, D. A. (2006). *It's Tough at the Top: The No-fibbing Guide to Leadership.* London: DSC.

Vaglum, P., Friis, S., & Karterud, S. (1985). Why are the results of milieu therapy for schizophrenic patients contradictory? An analysis based on four empirical studies. *Yale Journal of Biological Medicine, 13*: 349–361.

Varese, F., Smeets, F., Drukker, M., Lieverse, C., Lataster, T., Viechtbaur, W., Read, J., Van Os, J., & Bentall, R. P. (2012). Childhood adversities increase the risk of psychosis: A meta-analysis of patient control, prospective and cross-sectional cohort studies. *Schizophrenia Bulletin, 38*: 661–671.

Wagenborg, J. E. A., Tremeronti, G. W., Hesselink, A. J., & Koning, R. F. (1988). The follow-up project on psychotherapeutic communities: Design and preliminary results. *International Journal of Therapeutic Communities, 9*: 129–152.

Waxer, P. H. (1977). Short-term group psychotherapy; some principles and techniques. *International Journal of Group Psychotherapy, 27*: 33–42.

Weissman, M. M. (1975). The assessment of social adjustment. *Archives of General Psychiatry, 32*: 357–365.

Wilke, G. (1998). Oedipal and sibling dynamics in organisations. *Group Analysis, 31*: 269–281.

Winnicott, D. W. (1963). The mentally ill in your caseload. In: *The Maturational Processes and the Facilitating Environment* (pp. 217–229). London: Karnac, 1965.

Winnicott, D. W. (1963). *The Maturational Processes and the Facilitating Environment.* London: Karnac, 1990.

Winnicott, D. W. (1971). *Playing and Reality.* London: Pelican, 1974.

Yalom, I. D. (1970). *The Theory and Practice of Group Psychotherapy*. New York: Basic Books.

Yalom, I. D. (1983). *Inpatient Group Psychotherapy*. New York: Basic Books.

Yalom, I. D., & Leszcz, M. (2005). *The Theory and Practice of Group Psychotherapy (Fifth edition)*. New York: Basic Books.

# INDEX